THE DAY
SATAN CALLED

THE DAY SATAN CALLED

A TRUE ENCOUNTER WITH DEMON POSSESSION AND EXORCISM

BILL SCOTT

New York Boston Nashville

All scripture quotations, unless otherwise indicated, are taken from the New King James Version®. Copyright © 1982 by Thomas Nelson, Inc. Used by permission. All rights reserved.

Scripture passages marked NIV are from THE HOLY BIBLE, NEW INTERNATIONAL VERSION®, NIV®. Copyright © 1973, 1978, 1984, 2011 by Biblica, Inc.™ Used by permission. All rights reserved worldwide.

Scripture passages marked The Message are taken from *The Message*. Copyright © 1993, 1994, 1995, 1996, 2000, 2001, 2002. Used by permission of NavPress Publishing Group.

FaithWords
Hachette Book Group
237 Park Avenue
New York, NY 10017

www.faithwords.com

Printed in the United States of America

First Edition: October 2011

10 9 8 7 6 5 4 3 2 1

FaithWords is a division of Hachette Book Group, Inc.
The FaithWords name and logo are trademarks of Hachette Book Group, Inc.

Library of Congress Cataloging-in-Publication Data

Scott, Bill.
The day Satan called : a true encounter with demon possession and exorcism / Bill Scott. — 1st ed.
    p. cm.
Summary: "A riveting account of demon possession and its devastating impact on one family"—Provided by the publisher.
ISBN 978-0-89296-898-5
1. Demoniac possession. 2. Exorcism. 3. Scott, Bill. I. Title.
BT975.S39 2011
235'.4092—dc23
[B]   2011018100

Acknowledgments

The story you are about to read is nothing short of amazing. I want to thank God for the opportunity to experience what I did—even though there were events and moments I hope to never experience again, and would never wish on anyone. But through this journey I experienced God's love and power more fully in my life. His hand of protection and His guidance were what wrote this book in my life.

But even with divine inspiration, it takes more than one person to write a book—especially for me, a radio guy who would rather say it than put it on paper. Writing a book, I've discovered, is a team effort, and so I want to thank some special people who helped bring this about.

I want to thank all my family members who have been so encouraging—and patient—during the writing of this book. It was my wonderful wife, Janet, who first encouraged me to put my experiences on paper. She believed in the story and me and worked many hours writing and editing it with me.

I am grateful for my agent, Mark Gilroy. He didn't just sell a book proposal but was there to help me work through every aspect of the writing process.

I am also grateful for my editor, Joey Paul, from the

FaithWords division of the Hachette Book Group. He had great questions and insights that turned this into a better book than I could have ever crafted on my own. Most of all, he believed in me and the message of hope behind this incredible experience. He got the whole publishing staff to really get behind the book—even if a few outside the Christian publishing arena raised a few eyebrows.

Thank you to my friends who have been so supportive in this venture. Thanks to Barry and Linda Armstrong, Dr. Tim Clinton, and mentor Don Creech for believing in me. Big things can be accomplished when friends and family stand together.

Finally, thank you for buying this book. I really believe at the end of the story you'll better understand what we face in the spiritual realm, but even more important, you will more fully understand the depths and riches of God's love and power and how it can be activated in your life.

God Bless,

Bill Scott

Contents

Author's Note on Names and Places ix

Introduction: I'm Really Not Crazy xi

1. The Call 1

2. Today Is Not That Day 10

3. The Abandoned Building 20

4. Praying with a Witch 28

5. She Lives Inside Me 37

6. The Houseguest 48

7. Demons Go to Church 56

8. The Journey Begins 68

9. An Answer to Prayer 73

10. The Haunted House 82

11. What Was Under the Bed? 92

12. The Search for Roxanne 108

13. Something Bad Is Happening 118

14. Death Threats, Mad Cows,
and the Disappearing Witch 128

15. Will This Ever Stop? 141

16. Roxanne Returns   156

17. Space Travel and the Road Trip   164

18: The Answer Is Revealed   177

19. It's Over   186

20. I Still Have Questions   188

21. Another Call   196

Appendix: Ten Spiritual and Life Lessons   201

Notes   207

Author's Note on Names and Places

Lacey is the real name of the one who reached out to me on my call-in line and began this story for me. Beyond that, I have changed the names of most participants. When you read the last chapters of *The Day Satan Called,* you will better understand my desire to protect the identity and privacy of a central character in my story. I've also left out place-names for the same reason. The events and conversations are all true.

I'm Really Not Crazy

> We do not wrestle against flesh and blood, but against principalities, against powers, against the rulers of the darkness of this age, against spiritual hosts of wickedness in the heavenly places.
>
> —Ephesians 6:12

I never planned—or even wanted—to write this book.

It's been years since this event happened—an event that covered eighteen excruciating months of my life. I've shared it with only a few trusted individuals over the years. Frankly, I have been concerned that if people who don't know me well heard me tell this story, they would think I was crazy or mentally unstable. But my reluctance to share what happened to me was based on more than a fear that I wouldn't be believed.

During this event there were death threats that both the police and I took seriously. For eighteen months my home was no longer a sanctuary. I lived in constant fear but especially dreaded nightfall each and every day. Human and inhuman voices. Noises. Threats. Cursing. Blasphemies. Objects moving. Doors opening and clos-ing. Strange calls and visitors at work and home. The experience was simply too surreal and too painful to want to relive. For two decades I have felt it was best not to talk about my experiences to anyone outside a small circle of friends.

You would have to be crazy to try to tell others about something this bizarre—and I'm not crazy.

I understand if you are skeptical already. You might be thinking it's convenient that I shared my story with only a few select individuals—and then waited more than twenty years to put it in book form. True, I can't prove the details of my ordeal other than through the testimony of other people involved in the events at the time, but what I'm about to share with you really happened. It is my personal testimony, not an apologetic to prove the existence of the spiritual world, including demons.

For any doubters, I think I understand where you are coming from. As I relived those tumultuous moments through writing this book I, too, found it very hard to believe that these things really happened—and I was there.

A lot has to do with my upbringing. I grew up in a small, very conservative, Bible-believing and Bible-teaching church. I was taught to know and love God's Word. But there were two things we really didn't talk about much: the power of the Holy Spirit and demons. In other words, we didn't talk about the spirit world; at least not in the modern-day world. The only time I remember hearing about demons from the pulpit was when a missionary from Africa came to speak at our small church. It's not that my pastor and Sunday school teachers didn't believe in demons, it just wasn't their teaching emphasis. What the missionary shared was fine with them, but probably because the demons were in a far-off and exotic land and not the USA; certainly not the town I grew up in. The spirit world was simply not part of our world. So I never met anyone who had encountered demons. I never heard anyone speak of spiritual warfare. Your upbringing might be quite different from mine, but there is a good chance you were raised the same way on this point of ignoring the spirit world.

Even though I grew up hearing Ephesians 6:12 quoted many times—"We do not wrestle against flesh and blood, but against principalities, against powers, against the rulers of the darkness of this age, against spiritual hosts of wickedness in the heavenly places"—I just hadn't given much thought to demons. I wasn't looking for them. I didn't believe—and still don't believe—they are under every rock and hiding in every nook and cranny. I was an average guy who was just living a normal life.

Again, the story I am about to share is true and has not been embellished in any way to make it more scintillating and strange than it actually was. I don't believe I'm crazy, and the people around me today seem to concur. This is not a vision or a product of my imagination. It actually happened to me.

I will never forget the day Satan called...

THE DAY
SATAN CALLED

CHAPTER 1

The Call

It was the week before Halloween in the fall of 1988. It figures. Isn't that the time you would expect a story like mine to begin?

Actually, I wasn't expecting anything at all. For me Halloween was nothing more than a time for harvest festivals, passing out candy to adorable little kids who would troop up to the door in their cute little costumes, the occasional report of someone getting their car windows "soaped" or "egged"—but not a serious holiday with spiritual meaning. Other than some scary ads for movies on television, Halloween did not conjure up spooky feelings or dread. After all, I was a healthy, well-adjusted adult living in a flesh-and-blood world. Yes, I was a Christian and believed God's Spirit lived in my heart. I believed in angels and even demons, but more on a theoretical basis than as something I would ever face and experience.

I was never so wrong about anything in my life.

It was a typical Thursday morning as I began my normal routine, which was to head to the production studio to begin working on announcements that would play during my segment on the radio. I was a midday announcer and production director for a radio station that was located in and part of the largest church in North America at that time. The day seemed normal; production work, phone calls, short meetings, and preparing myself mentally for my shift.

A little before 10:00 a.m., I remember shuffling all the stuff on my desk into neat piles and then heading down the hall to the main studio where I would interact on live air for the next three hours. We had a great news team that worked across the hall. As I opened the door to enter my studio I saw Rick, the news director, hang up the request-line phone. I was a little surprised that he was over in the main studio and that he was answering my phone. As my friend turned around and faced me, I saw that all the color had drained from his face. You've heard of people going white as a ghost. I'll never again question what that means and looks like. I literally saw someone go white as a ghost. I was taken aback, and, strange for me, I was speechless. I wasn't sure what to say to him or even what to ask him. Rick sat there and looked at me for a minute, visibly shaken, and then said loudly and forcefully that he had just talked to a demon on the phone.

This brought me back to my senses. Now I knew it must really be the Halloween season and someone was trying to play a joke on me. So I belted out a loud courtesy laugh, ready to give him kudos for his great acting job. He really did look scared.

Rick just looked at me and said again, "I'm serious. I just talked to a demon on the phone, and I don't know what to do! We need to do something!"

Again I chuckled and told Rick that it was not real; it was just someone playing a prank. Besides, I wanted to ask him, how would he know that a demon had just called him on the phone?

But despite my protestations, Rick wasn't joking. He continued to say again and again that it was a demon and that we needed to help the girl who was calling us.

As I noted before, I grew up in a very strict independent Christian church, and if there was one thing we never talked about, it was the spiritual world. Of course we acknowledged the Holy Spirit, but even He was portrayed as a rather subdued character. I love the church that I grew up in, but I have wondered if we shouldn't have talked about spiritual warfare just a little bit. Spiritual victory was a matter of knowing God's Word—areas that might lead you astray because they were more tied to emotions were not studied but rather avoided. Some ministers from my tradition would go so far as to say that demons, like miracles, were restricted to biblical times and didn't exist in the present tense.

I stopped telling Rick that I knew he was joking, but I reminded him that it was the Halloween season, we were a Christian radio station, and that perhaps the newsroom didn't get prank phone calls, but we got them in the on-air studio all the time. It was just some kid home sick from school for the day who was bored and getting into some mischief. I knew when I was home as a schoolkid I could get into this kind of trouble. Prank calls were a staple of my growing-up years. What a great place to call— a radio station. You couldn't help thinking that maybe your crank call would make it onto the airwaves.

Rick ignored my disclaimers and insisted it was a real call from someone who was in desperate trouble; someone who was under the influence of a demon. I asked Rick how he knew it was a demon. Rick, who was growing more agitated and upset as we talked rather than calming down, said that he could tell it wasn't a human voice.

Rick had my attention by now. If he was playing a joke on me, he had taken it way too far. I knew him well enough to see that he was truly rattled in a way I had never seen him before. I finally concluded that he really did believe what he was saying to me. But I had never known anyone who had claimed to have talked to a demon in person, much less on the phone. Not even the missionary from Africa. I wasn't sure it was possible, so my mind was looking for other explanations of what Rick might have experienced.

Rick continued to explain to me that it was not a human that he talked to on the phone. He said that as soon as he heard the voice, every hair on his head stood on end. At this point I ran out of things to say. I knew Rick was sincerely scared, but based on my life experience, I didn't believe he had just talked to a demon. Why would a demon call my request line, anyway? I was most certain there wasn't a song in our library he would have wanted to hear.

As we stood behind the control board, at an impasse, I tried to lighten the atmosphere with another attempt at humor. Again I began to make fun of the call Rick had received. I was hoping my levity would settle Rick down and get him to think clearly. Though I had never seen him so upset and I was concerned, it was time for me to go on the air and Rick was just going to have to get over the call so I could get my job done.

The request line began to ring. Rick looked at me and pointed.

"Look," he said, "*you* answer it and see for yourself if I'm making something up."

While we had debated whether he had actually talked to a demon, Rick had told me that the call he took was from a sixteen-year-old girl named Lacey. She felt her life was in danger and was desperate for help. That's when the demon broke in and said he would kill her if Rick tried to help, and seconds later the line went dead. This flashed through my mind as the phone continued to ring. I just stared at it. There was no answering machine, so it rang until you picked it up. I have to admit, now I was a little scared. Rick looked at me, maybe with a trace of triumph in his expression, as I stared at the blinking request line.

Finally I gave my head a shake, told myself it was no big deal, and answered the phone. Little did I know that by answering that phone call that day, my life would be changed forever. It was like opening Pandora's box.

I picked up the receiver and said simply, "Hello?"

The voice I heard was weak, timid, and very scared. What sounded like a little girl began to talk to me. Rick, who had put his ear as near to the outside of the headset as he could, was listening intently. He looked at me and soundlessly mouthed, *That's her.*

I asked who was calling and what I could do for her. She told me her name was Lacey and that she needed help. For the next few minutes Lacey told me things that were shocking and that I thought just couldn't be true. She told me that she was living in a coven under strict watch and control. She described her life as if she were a prisoner. Being held prisoner by witches in twentieth-century America?

What I knew about covens came from literature and movies, but like the idea of present and active demons, I had never given any thought to them as something real. I read later that *coven* or *covan* is a word used to describe a gathering of witches or, in some cases, vampires. Vampires? I had watched some old Count Dracula movies in black and white as a kid. That's all I knew about vampires at the time. Vampires weren't the literary rage they became later through popular fiction authors.

I asked Lacey how old she was. She said that she was sixteen. After a pause, she told me the same thing she had told Rick: that she was very scared for her life. She went on to say the most horrifying thing imaginable. She said that she was to be sacrificed on Halloween and she didn't want to die. I was looking at Rick with absolute disbelief as I talked to Lacey on the phone. A part of me was very frightened, but I also had a fleeting thought that this was nothing more than a pre-Halloween prank by a teenager who liked to watch scary movies. But listening to her speak, I knew this was not someone trying to pull a hoax on us. I put Lacey on speakerphone so Rick could hear every word, too.

I wasn't sure I believed Lacey lived in a coven, but I believed she was frightened for her life. So I told her how much we cared for her and that we could get her the help she needed. I told her we could begin working to get her into a safe house. It was at that point I almost wet my pants. At first it sounded as though she were gagging on something. But then I heard a voice that was clearly not human. I don't have the words to describe what it sounded like. But like Rick, every hair on my body was standing on end. He and I looked at each other with eyes as wide as saucers. I had just heard the voice of a demon. Rick had been telling the truth.

You might wonder, if I had never heard a demon speak, how did I know I'd just heard one? All I can say is, when a demon speaks to you there is no doubt in your mind that you are in the presence of evil. It's more than the sense of sound. Every part of you experiences it physically and emotionally. Your mind does a somersault and both sharpens and blurs; your heart races but feels like it might stop; you can feel a palpable presence of evil tingling in your knees and elbows; your breathing becomes very shallow; a heaviness settles over your thoughts.

This is what I experienced—and it was something I had never experienced before. The sound literally took my breath away. In some cases, as I was soon to discover, the temperature in the room feels as though it has dropped to near freezing. That didn't happen, but there was no doubt this was a real spiritual encounter.

The demon stated that he was going to kill Lacey and there was nothing we could do to save her. He triumphantly stated that she belonged to Satan. He told us to stay away from her or we would suffer the consequences. Lacey came back on the line in tears, asking what was happening to her. She begged us to help her. My head was spinning. Lacey would speak and then the demon would break in to tell us we could not save her. Sometimes he would scream and yell curses and blasphemies at us.

Again, please remember I was never taught much about the reality of demons, much less how to deal with a demon. I was clueless. From the recesses of my childhood memories I did remember something the missionary who had spoken at our church had said. He told us how a Christian can bind Satan in Jesus' name. So I did what I thought would solve the problem. I yelled into the phone with as much courage as I could muster, "In Jesus' name, you must go! I bind you in Jesus' name." I'll never forget the response. It was not what I expected.

The demon, in a very quiet voice, said, "__ you, I am going nowhere."

Maybe I hadn't said it with enough conviction. Maybe it took more than one time to work. So with a little more courage and in an even louder voice I repeated, "In Jesus' name, you must go! I bind you in Jesus' name."

I received the same response from the demon on the phone. That was my very best effort at spiritual warfare.

We had drawn a small crowd of colleagues to the studio by this time. Sad to say, there wasn't anyone else around who had any more of a clue of what to do than I did. I didn't realize at the time that Satan will test you to see if you really know your power is in Christ alone. I learned firsthand and quickly that he will intimidate you and put a fear in you so that you believe there is nothing you can do.

In this case it worked.

Lacey hung up on us but called back just a little while later. This continued all day on Thursday until late in the evening. The phone calls would last for five minutes or so. I would talk to Lacey, then the demon, and the phone would go dead.

On one of her calls Lacey shared with me that when she was younger, the coven she was in had sacrificed her baby. I was stunned and incredulous, which I didn't think was possible after all I had already heard from her. She explained that she was a "breeder," and the witches used her and other young women to bear children so they would have babies to kill and even eat during certain satanic holidays. She told me she was born to be a breeder. She had not been allowed to go out in public and had never attended school.

We later discovered she had no birth certificate or other government identification so there was no record of her existence, much less of her having been pregnant or having a baby. I was horrified by everything she was telling me. I may not have believed in demons or satanic activity before, but I did now. I was terrified, but I am not the kind of guy who gives up very easily on people. And I wasn't going to give up on Lacey—though if I knew then what I know now, I might not have kept picking up the phone.

That was the day Satan called. I wasn't ready for it. Maybe it's not possible for anyone to be prepared for a jolt like that.

But God was present and working in and through me, despite my limited knowledge and feeble faith. So I resolved that no matter what, I would continue to pick up the phone. And with God's grace, I did.

CHAPTER 2

Today Is Not That Day

That first day I sat on the edge of my seat in the studio, phone pressed to my ear, all day and all evening. It felt like a watch vigil—everyone waiting anxiously in the studio for the next call from Lacey and the demon.

This entire time members of the staff at the radio station and church where we were located joined me around the phone, praying for this little girl who told us she was going to be sacrificed on Halloween. Between hang-ups and interruptions from the demon, I would ask Lacey questions about her surroundings, trying to figure out her location. It felt like I was searching for a drowning child with my eyes blindfolded.

She didn't know street or place-names, but through describing landmarks and a process of elimination, we finally figured out what nearby city she was living in. After a particularly fruitful round of questions, one of the church staff members thought he had her location pinpointed.

He and a few friends ran to the car, ready to race to a nearby town so they could swoop in to rescue her. We were all exhilarated. Adrenaline was pumping. Even those of us who stayed behind felt as though we were in the car with them. The end of this emotional ordeal was coming to a close. Talk about a change of pace at the office.

But euphoria quickly gave way to an exhausting tedium.

What started out as a rescue adventure proved to be a wild-goose chase. Every time the rescue team got close to where we thought Lacey was, she would describe a new location, a new landmark. What was going on? Was she confused? Was she being moved to new locations because others were aware she was on the phone with us? Did she not really want to be found?

You may have already wondered how someone in near-captivity could have so much access to a telephone. Looking back, it is easy to see that some things didn't add up. Not only did she have constant access to a phone, but she seemed to be constantly on the move. (This was the pre-cell-phone era, so it's not likely someone trapped in a house or out on errands with her captors could have un-limited and secret use of the phone.)

All I can say is there was such an urgency and such a bizarre vibe surrounding all this, none of us were able to slow down and figure out that maybe this little girl's intentions were not totally innocent and that she was per-haps making us out to be fools. After all, this had gone far beyond a church or Christian radio station prank, innocent or otherwise. We knew we were dealing with malignant evil, but at this point, we never suspected it might be coming from Lacey.

For seven or eight hours, we asked her questions about her location and did our best to communicate with the searchers. This turned into a monumental logistical task. The search-and-rescue team had to stop to find a pay phone constantly, turning their efforts into a stop-and-start haphazard run through a maze.

The demon knew what we were trying to do and would interrupt my talks with Lacey to taunt me. He told me that he would move her every time we got anywhere close to her. He said we would never find her. He thought this was funny and would laugh hysterically. It was late Thursday night and our team was nowhere close to locating Lacey. Then Lacey's phone calls stopped. What an anticlimactic end to a heart-pounding, breathtaking day.

Driving home that night, I was trying to figure out exactly what had just happened to me. Questions swirled around in my mind. Could I have really talked with a demon and someone who was being held captive in a coven? Had we lost Lacey for good? And even if we found her, would we be able to save her life?

I prayed myself to sleep that night.

As I drove to work on Friday, the same questions bounced around in my head like a rubber ball in a concrete room. I wondered if I would ever talk to Lacey again. Was she gone forever? My world had been shaken.

I arrived at the office early. The phones were being carefully monitored. No calls from Lacey. My day almost began to feel normal as I strode down the hall a little before 10:00 a.m. toward the main studio to start my on-air shift. But the closer I got to the door, the more apprehension and anxiety I felt. I shrugged the feeling away and entered the soundproof room and took my seat. I wasn't behind the control board more than a minute when the phone rang.

Could it be Lacey? Suddenly afraid, I allowed the phone to ring a few extra times before I found the courage to pick up the headset. I had made a commitment to see this strange conversation through to the end, so I answered.

"This is Bill Scott."

What I heard was that pitiful little girl, pleading and crying for me to help her, to save her life. My heart was broken at the sound of her sobbing.

The pattern from the previous day resumed. I would talk to Lacey, the demon would cut in to scream at me, and then the phone would go dead. How I managed to do my show while this drama churned and spun around me, I will never know.

Throughout the day Lacey told me of abuse she had experienced, from giving up her baby for a sacrifice to being sexually molested. Could all the things she was describing have really happened? Did this kind of coven actually exist? My natural doubts and skepticism were held at bay each time the demon would break in and scream, cuss, laugh at me, and speak all kinds of evil and blasphemy against Jesus Christ. I had never felt this kind of oppression, this level of evil directed at my life. Again, every hair on my body stood on end each time he came on the phone.

One thought that kept working itself around my mind was that whoever had hurt this little girl needed to spend time in prison. I was beginning to feel anger, which was a good antidote to the prevailing sense of fear and dread I had experienced the previous day.

Beyond anger, to my pleasant surprise, the longer I dealt with this demon, the more confident I became. The Holy Spirit was ministering to me and giving me words and an authority I had never felt before. I have to repeat that I could never have done this had it not been for a number of people around me praying as I talked with Lacey and the demon.

At one point the demon, in a much quieter voice, asked me to go away and not try to help Lacey anymore. It was almost like he was making a request or asking a favor. I said to him, "You have to obey the power of Christ." Everyone in the room was silent when the demon replied: "One day my knee will bow and my tongue will confess that Jesus is Lord."

We were nearly breathless. We looked at one another with a new confidence. We felt lighter and stronger.

Then he screamed, "But today is not that day."

We jumped in our chairs and our heads jerked back in unison as a mocking laugh morphed into a pitch that sounded as if he was being tormented. The phone went dead again.

I stayed on the phone with Lacey that day as long as the line stayed open, while several teams went back out in cars, following clues and searching for her. This ordeal had been going on for only twenty-four hours, but we were beginning to feel fatigued and weary. It wasn't just tiredness of body, but also of the soul. While talking to Lacey and battling the demon that would speak through her, what kept me going was the people coming and going and praying over me.

Susan, who worked at the church as a secretary, had an office just up the hall from where the radio station was located within the church. She had been home that day, but when she heard what we were experiencing, she called and said she would drive over as quickly as she could to pray for us and with us. She told us she had been involved in a number of occult groups years before. She had witnessed and practiced witchcraft before experiencing a dramatic conversion through Jesus Christ, she explained. Her heart ached for Lacey, and she wanted to help us rescue her in any way she could.

I told Susan that up to this point I had been unable to get Lacey to say Jesus' name in the course of our conversations. Lacey just could not get that word out, even when she seemed to be trying. A few times it felt like she was getting close, but then the demon would break in once again, cursing, scoffing, and berating me and anyone else in the room. Each time he would emphatically say that we could not have Lacey and that he would not leave. Susan was confident that Lacey's resistance and the demon's anger were signs that she was taking very seriously the call to turn her life over to God through Jesus Christ. She said she'd come to the church immediately.

The fact that we would be joined with someone more knowledgeable on satanic activity than any member of the team was a confidence booster for us. I felt immediately better when I got word that Susan had arrived. Susan walked into the room during a particularly intense encounter with the demon. As she closed the door behind her, the demon got very quiet but didn't break off the connection. It was so quiet you could have heard a pin drop. Usually such silence was quickly followed by the phone being slammed down. Susan looked around, sensing that we were in the midst of a big moment. We stared at one another. We could barely breathe; then suddenly yet calmly the demon spoke: "Susan, it's good to see you again. We've missed you."

I was dumbfounded. I almost fell out of my seat. No

one from the small group gathered around me had mentioned Susan by name or even acknowledged her when she came into the room. Yet this demon knew she had entered the room and recognized her.

The blood drained from Susan's face and she stared at the phone. She gave a little shake of her head, turned around quickly, and ran out the door, bursting into tears.

The sense of confidence I had felt burst like a bubble.

After Susan had some time to pull herself back together after the shock of hearing her name called out by a demon, she returned to pray with us and for Lacey. She was not going to allow Satan to defeat her as he had previously. Susan knew as a child of God that she had the power to face spiritual battle and win. I'm sure she also identified with Lacey and wanted to see someone else brought from the darkness and into the light of God's love.

Even though the quick surge of confidence I had experienced with the word that we would have an experienced helper was dashed, we all began to feel a subtle but more sure form of courage. We began to understand that our success would depend not on the state of our emotions at any given moment, but on our confidence in God's love and power.

New thoughts and questions joined others that were already racing around in my mind. Was this really happening? How did a demon talk on the telephone and how did this demon know what was going on in our studio? Were we going to win? Could we save Lacey?

Words seem inadequate to describe the way I felt. It is an experience that I would not wish on anyone. This was the most emotionally and physically draining sensation I have ever known.

I knew that I didn't know what I was doing and that we were undoubtedly not handling everything correctly, but we were doing our best and we were going to fight for this girl who was going to die unless we helped her. Yes, I had finally come to believe her situation was real, not just in her imagination. How can you quit fighting when you know someone's life is on the line? I couldn't.

Day two of being on the phone with Lacey and the demon was going much like the first day. I was mentally and emotionally drained. We all were.

But to make our physical and emotional states worse, in addition to all that was going on with Lacey, we had to put the final touches on a huge concert sponsored by the radio station to be held that night. Our worship center would be filled with thousands of people in just a few hours.

I suspected our high visibility as a media outlet, as a large church, and as a Christian event center was the reason Lacey knew about us and chose to call us in the first place.

Throughout the day Lacey continued to phone my line, crying out for help. My heart was consumed with the thought of saving this young woman. Each time we talked I would tell her of God's unconditional love for her. She had a hard time comprehending this. It was obvious from her questions and responses that she believed love was something given to you by others only when they wanted something sexual. When I told her God's love and my love and the love of those praying for her had nothing to do with sex, she would respond that I was lying and trying a new trick to seduce her. Her life experiences had followed a very set pattern: She was treated badly most of the time, but on occasions when someone said they cared for her, they were always trying to get her in a better mood for having sex. Again and again I assured her that my friends and I who were praying for her loved her, and we didn't want anything from her, sexual or otherwise.

I had never talked to or heard of anyone who had withstood as much abuse as Lacey described. Nobody who went through what she had could survive without mental illness. But there was no question in my mind that she was also possessed by a demon or many demons. I had never knowingly met a witch, and now I was talking to a girl who claimed to live in a coven, claimed to be a witch, claimed to be a priestess of Satan, and claimed to be intimately involved in a number of satanic rituals: cutting one's own flesh, drinking blood from humans and animals, sexual rituals too disgusting to mention, and even human sacrifice.

My head continued to spin. This was a lot for a fairly sheltered Baptist boy to process in just two fast-paced and headlong days. But I wasn't going to allow what I didn't know or understand to cause me to give up on this young woman.

Late that afternoon Lacey asked me about the concert that was going to be held at the church that night. Obviously she was listening to our radio station. I held out little hope that she would actually come, but I invited her to be our guest at the concert anyway. I was willing to try just about anything that would get her away from her situation and the people causing it. What better place to meet could there be than a church? A holy place. If we could get her into our building, we might be able to talk to her freely and perhaps get her whatever help she needed.

I was surprised when she said she would come if she could. But I still didn't think she would make it. If her situation was as chaotic as we thought, we could go to her, but how would she come to us?

Who knew that after all the frantic searching we had done over the past forty-eight hours that finally meeting Lacey in person would be as simple as inviting her to a concert.

The invitation set the stage for us to meet Lacey. But it was anything but "simple."

CHAPTER 3

The Abandoned Building

It was now evening. It was hard to believe that I had been on the phone for a second day talking with Lacey and whomever and whatever else was inside her.

I knew from reading Scripture and hearing lessons and sermons growing up that King Saul had met with a witch before going to his final battle (1 Sam. 28:7). I knew that Jesus and His disciples cast out demons.

But never in my wildest dreams would *I* have anticipated personally doing battle with a demon. Maybe a missionary in Africa. But not Bill Scott.

However, that's exactly what I had done all day while on the phone with Lacey. I was cursed at and ridiculed, but I soldiered on, quoting Scripture and relying on the power of Jesus' name and the prayers of my brothers and sisters in Christ. The demon swore we would never save Lacey, which only strengthened our resolve. We had been given a supernatural love for a young girl we had never met that would not let us stop.

It was about an hour before the concert was to start. Based on previous events we sponsored, we were expecting more than three thousand people that evening and the parking lot was already filling up. Our church was a huge structure. The sanctuary alone was 150 yards wide, the length of one and a half football fields. Our custo-dial staff piloted riding vacuum cleaners in order to keep up with the demands of cleaning the vast building. The entire church campus was huge, which is very important to note in order to understand everything that happened next.

I hadn't spoken with Lacey for two hours. I didn't know if she was going to come to the concert or not. Maybe she would change her mind. Maybe she couldn't get free of the people who had such an iron grip on her life.

Everyone was on high alert for a young teenage girl who looked distressed. Not much to go on as a descrip-tion, but it was all we had from our phone conversations. Our staff was prepped and ready to meet her. The church security personnel were alerted to what was going on in case there was a confrontation. The decision had been made, wisely, to contact the local police, and they had officers present. People went through the motions of doing their part to make sure everything was perfect for the concert, but our minds and hearts were elsewhere. All that we could do now was watch, wait, and pray.

Finally the call-in line rang. It was Lacey. She told me she was close to the church. I could feel my heart pound-ing as I talked to her. I was now used to the inevitable interruption as the demon broke in. His pattern hadn't changed. He cursed at me and blasphemed Jesus Christ. He scoffed at my weak attempts to save Lacey. He then said something that caught my attention even more. He said that his people would kill Lacey at the concert if she made it as far as the church doors. His people? What did that mean? Who were they?

He told me that witches had been summoned from all over the area to snatch Lacey before she could cross the threshold of the church. The demon kept repeating that Lacey was to be their sacrifice and that we would never save her.

We were prepared to meet a young teenage girl, not an assault of witches, armed police officers notwithstanding. To state the obvious, this was the craziest situation and moment of my life. No way could it get crazier. Right? I was wrong again.

The call ended, but Lacey rang back almost immediately. I asked her to describe her location. From what she told me I realized she was just a mile up the road at a local ice-cream shop. A couple of staff members dashed out the door and hopped in a car to drive over and pick her up. We waited almost breathlessly for them to return with her. But ten minutes later they called from the shop to report she wasn't there. They had looked everywhere, including the women's restroom. My frustration was mounting. Another false lead? Another wild-goose chase?

I talked to Lacey again briefly, but she hung up abruptly. That wasn't the usual pattern. Usually it was the demon that slammed down the phone in my ear.

What did this mean? Had she been found by members of the coven? I was ready to explode. How could we be so close to finding her only to be thwarted again? Was our fight a lost cause? I didn't have to wait long for answers to my questions, though it felt like a lifetime.

About thirty excruciating minutes later I received a call from an extension inside the church. I wondered who from the station or church staff would be calling me right now, particularly since I was keeping the line open for Lacey and everyone knew it. Had someone from the church found her? I answered the phone quickly. It was Lacey. No one had found her, but she was inside the church building. I would have let out a victory whoop, but suddenly she was screaming for help. Then the demon let out a scream of protest on the line. Knowing she was in a church made the demon's voice all the more chilling and threatening. The phone was slammed down. Almost instantly, my line rang from another inside extension. I picked up. It was Lacey crying for help, quickly followed by the demon shrieking we couldn't have her, and the phone again being slammed down.

This same unreal pattern was repeated several times. What in the world was going on? I picked up my phone yet again. But it wasn't Lacey this time. The church receptionist wanted to know what was going on and why so many people from inside the building were calling me. I told her it was just one person, Lacey, the girl we had been trying to connect with.

She said, "Bill, I don't think that's possible. It can't be just one person. Your phone is being called from different extensions all over the church building!"

Lacey was calling from one end of the church to the other end just seconds apart. She was calling from phones that were in locked offices. Remember what I said about the size of our church building? It would take a normal person five minutes to walk from one extension to the next. It was impossible for her to be calling from all these extensions seconds apart.

Once again—and not for the last time—I felt the hair on my head standing on end. I knew it was impossible for what was happening to be happening. But even the remaining skeptic inside me knew that I was not dealing with flesh and blood, but with spiritual forces, dark forces, and a power that was truly satanic.

While I answered my phone as quickly as Lacey could call it, I wasn't the only one from our group who was busy. Someone came back to where I was working the phone to tell me that people had begun to show up at the entrance door of the radio station, asking the workers where they could find Lacey. Suspicious and on guard, one of our group leaders asked what this was about. He was told, "She is one of us and we want to take her home."

One of us? Did this mean members of her coven were here? Witches? Demon-possessed individuals who blended into their communities when not practicing their dark rituals? Even as I asked myself those questions I wondered again if I was going out of my mind. Could all this really be happening? One of my favorite bands was already playing, but a night I had looked forward to for months was turning into the culmination of a nightmare. How had I found myself in a cheap horror movie? I looked down the hall and saw security and the police officer escorting what had to be the self-proclaimed witches out of the building. Lacey was in the building, and true to the demon's promise, his people had shown up to take her away and kill her or whatever else they had planned for her. I thought to myself that things could not get any stranger, but, once again, I was wrong.

Lacey called one more time that night. She said she wanted to meet me and me alone.

Behind our church was an old empty building, a retirement center that had been closed for years. It also had an old morgue inside. We had joked from time to time that the building was haunted. Our lighthearted attempts at humor didn't seem very funny at the moment. All that was missing was pipe organ music in the background.

I knew where she wanted to meet before she said it. I just knew. As I look back, I think I had already started walking there when Lacey said to meet her on the porch of the retirement center. It was already dark outside and the abandoned building wasn't lit. I trudged forward. There was just enough glow from the main church building to see where I was walking but not enough to see what was ahead. Yet here I was, walking away from the back of our main building to meet a witch. My thoughts went back to King Saul. Wasn't he killed and beheaded shortly after meeting the Witch of Endor?

I kept asking myself, *Why am I doing this?*

But I had told Lacey that we loved her and would do all we could to see that she was safe. Several of our group members didn't think meeting her at an abandoned building was such a good idea—including my wife—and that this was going beyond the promise to do "all we could do."

As I walked out of our building I reminded them that we had asked God to give us an opportunity to save Lacey's life, and this seemed to be it.

To be honest, I agreed with the objections. I didn't think it was such a good idea either. Even though I didn't think of myself as a particularly brave man, bottom line, I hadn't worked this hard to give up now. Maybe this was where I discovered my greatest strength as a Christian: spiritual stubbornness.

I strode across the lawn and down a lane lined with trees toward the old retirement building. But I didn't look or feel like John Wayne or Clint Eastwood heading out to meet the bad guys for a gunfight. I could feel my knees shaking sideways—I now knew what "knocking knees" meant. It wasn't just a figure of speech. I was officially terrified! As I approached the old run-down retirement center, I could see the outline of a person on the porch. It had to be Lacey. But would she still be there when I got to the porch? Would she be alone? Was this a trap? Was she working for the demon I had been battling for more than a day? I had already wondered that when things she said on the phone didn't add up.

I was awake and alert, but at the same time extremely fatigued. My mind was sharp and clear, but I was in a daze. Each step felt like it took a half hour.

I had experienced so much evil over the last thirty-four hours that I was at the end of my mental and emotional rope. I just knew I had to do this somehow. I had to keep putting one foot in front of the other. I prayed for God to give me strength so I could make it to the porch and talk with Lacey. The closer I got, the more I could hear my heart pounding.

I saw a movement in the shadows of the porch and called out, "Lacey."

At that point I saw something that still gives me the creeps to this day. The figure of the person began to walk and then run across the porch. The last thing I saw was her shadow run right into a brick wall and disappear. She was gone.

I froze for just a second and then I turned and ran like a frightened child for the safety of the church. I was gasping for breath by the time I arrived at the back entrance of the radio station annex. There were a number of people, including my wife, anxiously waiting and watching for me to return. No doubt, one look at my face and they knew something was wrong. But I didn't say a thing. I was out of breath, but I think I was also in a near state of shock. I hustled past all of them and a growing cadre of security guards to what felt like the safety of my office. I was still trembling when a small group of friends entered behind me. It took a couple of minutes to catch my breath, and then I told them what had just happened.

Everyone was amazed, but no one was more amazed than me. The whole experience just seemed so surreal, it was like watching a bad movie or having a bad nightmare. But there was just no mistaking it; what had happened was real.

And it wasn't over.

CHAPTER 4

Praying with a Witch

I had walked to the abandoned building behind our church and seen a figure run through a brick wall. I had raced back to the church and my friends. My breathing had returned to normal. I took stock of where we were in trying to help Lacey.

The fact was, we couldn't find her. We may have felt that we were close enough to touch her, but we really didn't know that for sure. As hard as we tried, maybe we weren't going to be able to meet with Lacey after all.

The concert played on with no sign of Lacey, and the phone just sat there, silent. For a second I sensed Lacey was back in the building, but I didn't know if that was true or not. How could I? We just knew she had stopped calling. The staff and I hung out in the lobby of the radio station, hoping for even one more chance to meet with her. We prayed. We talked and speculated. Perhaps someone did capture her while she was trying to reach out to us for help. We discussed the mystery of how someone who was a borderline prisoner was seemingly able to use a phone and move about freely. But the supernatural physical manifestations surrounding this drama—nonhuman voices and then the calls from the various areas of the church tonight—proved to us there was a malignant spiritual presence at work in the life of this young girl.

I don't think I was the only one who felt defeated. And maybe I wasn't the only one who felt a little relieved, too. I had tried my hardest and it wasn't good enough. We all had. Now the ordeal would end and life would go back to normal. In a month or two, all this would be forgotten.

While idly waiting, another witch came to the radio station. How did we recognize that she was a witch? Simple. She told us she was. A friend brought back a young woman in her early to mid-thirties asking for Lacey.

The woman introduced herself to us as Roxanne, and immediately looked straight at me and asked what I had done with Lacey. She wanted to know where I last saw her, why she had come to see me in particular, and if anything unusual had happened.

I answered her questions with questions of my own, most notably, who was she and what did she want with Lacey? Roxanne was evasive but finally blurted out that she had to find Lacey because she had been given a special assignment. I asked her several times what the assignment was, and after a lot of persistent badgering, she finally answered, "I think you know."

"Maybe I do, but I want to hear it from you," I answered.

"I've come to kill her," Roxanne said in a matter-of-fact tone, as if she were telling me she had come to borrow a cup of sugar or return a book I had lent her.

We were shocked. The fact that she spoke the words with no emotion at all made it more chilling than if she had screamed it with anger and rage. I know now what is meant by the phrase "cold-blooded killer."

We were scared and nervous and alert—despite the advantage of safety in numbers. A couple of us kept looking toward the door, wondering if one of the security guards or police officers was still present in our part of the building. I had studied her as discreetly as possible, and she didn't seem to be carrying any weapons. As we continued to talk in normal but guarded tones, Roxanne asked me again what Lacey wanted with us. I told her that she wanted to know more about God and His love. I told Roxanne that we all cared deeply about Lacey and wanted to help her, to see her become a child of God. We wanted to make sure she was safe.

As I said this Roxanne became nervous and agitated. I took this as a sign that my words were hitting the mark with her as well. She stood up and started pacing back and forth as several of us continued to talk about the love of Jesus Christ. She appeared not to be listening. But she wasn't leaving the studio either. It felt to me that she, too, wanted to hear more about this God who loved witches, who loved Lacey, who might even love Roxanne. But it was almost as if she couldn't bear to hear the words. So she paced and mumbled.

Then all at once she seemed to relax. She plopped down in a chair and began to tell us she had been involved in sacrifices, given up her own babies for the coven, drank the blood of animals, and participated in many other rituals. I thought I was hearing Lacey's story all over again. Just how many victims were tied to this coven?

We responded to Roxanne in the only way we knew how. We continued to talk about the love of God and His power to make us new creatures. I still remember quoting 2 Corinthians 5:17 to her: "If anyone is in Christ, he is a new creation; old things have passed away; behold, all things have become new."

We couldn't have prepared ourselves for what happened next.

Suddenly a man's voice rumbled out of Roxanne. We flinched and looked at one another in fear and amazement. Had we just heard this? Once again, I was sure I had lost my mind. Demons. Witches. Covens. Rituals. And now right before my eyes, a man's voice, not a deep woman's voice, but a deep man's voice was coming from the lips of a petite woman. I could feel the evil. I was in the presence of a demon. Talking to a demon on the phone had been terrifying, but this was even worse.

Roxanne's eyes rolled back in her head until we saw only the whites; her face contorted and became disfigured. It was her, but I'm not sure we would have said it was the same person if she had first left and then walked back in with her face physically twisting and morphing. The voice boomed at us. Like the demon that had spoken through Lacey on the phone, he cursed, blasphemed, scoffed at us for thinking we could make him leave, and in the most menacing voice I have ever heard, restated that Lacey belonged to him.

"You will never have her. She is mine."

The room grew silent and Roxanne went limp. Then she spoke in her normal voice. It was as if nothing extraordinary had just happened, and she was simply moving to the next sentence from where she left off previously. She continued her haunting story. She said that she grew up in the coven and was a high priestess. I heard her repeat many of the same life details that Lacey had given, but they were even more cutting and troubling because now the person telling them was standing in front of us and not at the end of a phone line. I wondered again just how many young women this coven had enslaved.

Then Roxanne said that she wanted to know more about Jesus Christ. This was a surprise. No, it was a shock. It came out of left field. And she said it so calmly. This was the first time she had spoken the name of Jesus, something Lacey had not done.

I shared with Roxanne more about God's love and His mercy and how He had died to take away the sins of the world. The more passionate I became, the more agitated the forces at war within her became. No longer calm, I was afraid we were losing Roxanne. Her eyes rolled back in her head again and now not just one, but many demon voices rushed out of her. They were all different and unique in sound.

Roxanne's emotions escalated. She got up and ran out into our small reception area and then back into the conference room. She bumped into things and fell down and got back up and did the same movements again. I stood to catch her to try to prevent her from hurting herself, but she immediately darted out of my reach. Honestly, I don't know what I would have done if I had caught her.

Then suddenly the temperature in the room dropped dramatically. It had been about seventy degrees. It was as if someone had pushed a button that could lower the room temperature instantaneously.

The temperature might actually have dropped, or perhaps we were experiencing just how cold evil actually is when you stand in its presence. It's a cold you cannot explain; it feels like it's coming from the inside out. Everyone in the room felt it.

But the cold was immediately forgotten when Roxanne let out a bloodcurdling scream, as though the demons were tormenting her. It hurt me to hear her in such pain. I couldn't imagine what she was feeling. I had never experienced anything remotely close to spiritual warfare in my entire life. Now I was a front-row witness to the wrath of evil forces.

While this was happening with Roxanne, I didn't have time to think about Lacey. The confrontation with Roxanne was now all-consuming. And it went on long after the concert was over, past midnight and into the morning hours. I would watch Roxanne as she looked at the ceiling and screamed, with multiple voices streaming from her at the same time. You've heard of heavenly choirs of angels. This was the exact opposite. It was a cacophony of evil and hatred spewing out at the world.

My boss from the radio station, James, was with us now. He had been involved in spiritual warfare before and took the lead in commanding the demons to leave Roxanne. Then the temperature seemed to return to where it had been just a moment earlier. Or perhaps we were just getting used to the evil that surrounded us.

James stopped talking. But the demon continued: "We will never leave her." James told them they must leave in the name of Jesus. Then they began to beg him not to cast them out.

One demon almost whimpered, "If I come back without this soul, my eternal torment will begin immediately."

Was I really hearing these things? Some of the voices of demons would go quiet—we assumed they had left—

but then there were new voices, new demons, entering Roxanne right behind the ones that had departed. How many demons could be in this girl? How would we ever get through them and subdue them long enough to see Roxanne set free by God's love?

This became our prayer: "Oh, God, give Roxanne peace and freedom from the demons so she can hear and respond to Your love for her."

In the middle of the night, a suddenly calm Roxanne looked at us and said she had decided to give her life to Christ. We were astonished. We felt so much relief and joy and gratitude as we bowed our heads to lead her in a prayer of repentance and acceptance of Jesus Christ as her Lord and Savior. We were amazed that our spiritual work with Roxanne seemingly had prevailed and was almost done. But our feeling of accomplishment was premature. Screams of fear and rage poured out of her, with different voices than before and now the sounds of animals added.

We battled on. It took another hour of what felt like hand-to-hand combat before Roxanne finally prayed the sinner's prayer and at James' leading said the words: "Jesus is my Lord."

There is power in the name of Jesus. I believed that then and I believe that now. I would stake my life on this promise from Scripture: "You are of God, little children, and have overcome them, because He who is in you is greater than he who is in the world" (1 John 4:4).

But it seemed we were not finished. We saw what looked like invisible demons physically pushing and pulling at Roxanne. She threw herself—and was thrown—all over the room. She passed out several times. Demons continued to scream and speak from her.

Whenever I had heard stories of a dramatic conversion to Christianity, salvation came instantly when the sinner's sincere prayer was offered. I believed Roxanne meant what she prayed. I was convinced she was sincere. So why were demons still at war inside her? When was this prayer going to prove the truth of Paul's well-known statement to the Roman church?

> *In all these things we are more than conquerors through Him who loved us. For I am persuaded that neither death nor life, nor angels nor principalities nor powers, nor things present nor things to come, nor height nor depth, nor any other created thing, shall be able to separate us from the love of God which is in Christ Jesus our Lord. (Romans 8:37–39)*

At seven in the morning, things had calmed down. Maybe the battle was over. Roxanne said she was ready to leave and go to a friend's home in the next town. She felt she would be safe with her. I have to admit, we were sluggish in our thinking at this point. I was feeling punch-happy. Everyone who had been up all night was listless and working hard to stifle yawns. If I had been sharper at this moment, I would have asked more questions about her friend, but Roxanne said she would be safe, so we let it go without a thought.

Yet there were so many things that didn't add up. Red flags were appearing everywhere. The fact that Roxanne had a safe place to go was a clear sign that not everything Lacey had told us about the situation in her coven was exactly as she described. At least it wasn't that way for Roxanne, who appeared to have a life outside an evil satanic group. I offer no excuses, but would simply note that everything we experienced was new territory and incredibly intense.

The one thing that was unquestionable was the reality of evil forces at work in these ladies' lives.

The group who had battled for Roxanne all night was truly exhausted. Wow, what an experience, what a battle, but praise God, we had won. Or so we thought. We all held hands with Roxanne, who was now part of the circle. Each of us prayed for God's protection on her life. I said a prayer for Lacey on behalf of the whole group as well. We hadn't heard from her in almost twelve hours. I prayed that God's angels would surround and protect her. We had no idea if Lacey had ended up attending the concert and got spiritual help there or returned to the coven on her own or had been abducted. We all left to go home and call it a night.

We tried to bring Lacey's whereabouts up with Roxanne once or twice, but she was so besieged with her own battle that she seemed to be in no condition to think of anyone else. We let it go.

What a day. What a night.

Who ever starts a week thinking they will encounter a demon-possessed girl? Watch a figure run through a brick wall at an abandoned nursing home? Be cursed and ridiculed nonstop for two days? Meet a witch? Pray with a witch?

All this had happened to me. But my week wasn't over.

CHAPTER 5

She Lives Inside Me

My wife and I went directly to bed. We were too exhausted to speak about the experiences of the evening. We just drove home silently, fell into bed, and drifted into a restless slumber. We hadn't slept very long when the phone rang. It was just 9:00 a.m. I groaned. I had barely gotten an hour of sleep.

It was Alan, a staff member at the radio station. He said Lacey had called looking for me and Roxanne was also calling for me. I did wonder why I was being singled out. I thought maybe James was front and center in the battle at this point.

But I jumped out of bed, threw on a pair of jeans and a sweatshirt, and headed back to the radio station. As I walked into the reception area Alan just stared at me, his face very pale and his expression frightened.

"Bill, you are not going to believe this," he said.

Now wide awake, I looked at him quizzically.

"Both Lacey and Roxanne have been calling me."

I already knew that. I asked him what was going on.

Alan said he just got off the phone with Roxanne, and Roxanne had asked if Lacey was okay. That was strange. Roxanne had come to the church looking for Lacey last night—to take her back to the coven, in fact—but once we had prayed with her, she would not even acknowledge her name.

Alan said he asked Roxanne if she knew Lacey. After a long pause Roxanne had said, "Yes." Then he asked if Roxanne knew where Lacey was right now and again Roxanne answered, "Yes," after another long pause.

"How do you know?" he asked her. "Where is she?"

Roxanne had told him, "She's here."

"How did she get there?" Alan asked, wondering how she got over to Roxanne's friend's house.

"She came with me," she answered.

"You picked her up on the way over this morning?" he asked.

Alan said there was another long pause where he wondered if he had lost the connection, so he repeated his question.

Alan was ashen as he told me her response.

"She lives inside me," she had told him.

"What?" he had choked out, wanting to make sure he understood her correctly.

Roxanne said again: "She lives inside me. She's a familiar spirit."

As Alan told me this, I was dumbfounded. A familiar spirit? Lacey wasn't real? At least not a real person? That couldn't be. After all, I had spent the last two days and the better part of two nights trying to share God's love with her. She had to be human. This seemed like such a cruel joke. Was this what the demon was laughing about when he taunted us over and over about never letting go of Lacey?

Could Lacey really be a demon?

I was crushed. Despite Roxanne's prayer to receive

Jesus Christ into her life, I felt defeated all over again. My mind quickly worked back through conversations with Lacey and the demon. I tried to tick off what I knew for sure, which wasn't much!

Had someone sincerely asked for help? If Lacey was a demon, then the answer was no, unless Roxanne was trying to reach us through someone she thought to be a "friendly spirit."

Had Roxanne become a Christian the night before? What if she had a split personality? Could one part of her be saved and another part still be demon-possessed?

Most of all I think I was feeling sorry for myself. How could I have spent so much time and prayer on Lacey, only to find out she was a spirit, and that she was not even savable? Why did things continue to be so confusing and difficult?

This was all racing through my mind in an instant. I thought about all we had gone through in the last few days. I had seen witches enter my church, trying to kidnap Lacey while we tried to protect her. I had spoken with demons. I had witnessed more than one demon speak and scream from the same person at the same time. I heard animal sounds coming from a human. I had been in a room when the temperature dropped to what felt like freezing. I had watched as Roxanne's eyes rolled up into the back of her head and she thrashed around as demons spoke out of her. I saw the shadow of Lacey run across a porch right into a brick wall and disappear.

It did cross my mind that if she were indeed a spirit, that would explain how she was able to pass through a brick-and-mortar wall. But that was only one mystery possibly solved.

Alan was looking at me, waiting for an answer. I shook my head slowly. None of this made sense. My thoughts went to my own well-being. Why had Lacey wanted to meet with me in particular? Was it to kill me? Inhabit me? Possess me? Was I a spiritual target? Had the forces of evil sensed a weakness in me that could be exploited?

I was really having a tough time trying to figure everything out. Even if Alan weren't waiting for an answer and I had hours to work on this, I don't think I would have been any further along on the road to understanding.

How do you go from being raised in a small independent church that doesn't really talk about spiritual warfare to witnessing everything I had in the last few days? I felt no doubt that what I had experienced was real. I just couldn't explain it.

In the weeks and months and even years to follow I was afraid to share this experience with people who weren't there. I really thought folks would think I was nuts. Maybe that's a big part of the reason why this book comes more than twenty years after the events. A couple of months later, I finally called my dad, a pastor in Tampa, Florida, to share what I had experienced. He told me a number of times that if what he was hearing was coming from anyone other than his own son, he would not have believed a word of it.

Standing face-to-face with Alan, all I wanted was to call for a time-out in order to work through this in my mind. Basketball coaches get to call a time-out when the situation on the court gets overwhelming. Why not a time-out when life gets overwhelming? I wanted time to process what I had experienced. But the situation with Roxanne was still happening in fast-forward.

Here is one thing I did think through quickly: If Lacey was indeed a satanic spirit, she had to be cast out of Roxanne for Roxanne to experience God's love and forgiveness and healing in her life. If Lacey was a split personality from Roxanne—the concept of multiple personalities was just becoming popular at that time—then I was way out of my depth to understand causes and effects and relationships—and there was nothing more I could do to help Roxanne. We would probably have to seek professional psychiatric support and care.

But based on the multiple inhuman voices pouring out of the same person, based on a person calling from different phones just seconds apart, based on the demon's knowledge of what was happening in our studio without being there, based on the temperature in the studio dropping dramatically—and based on the physical and emotional impact that phone conversations had on each and every one of our group members—I was convinced Lacey was much more than a splinter personality. Lacey was actually a demon. It was not Roxanne who had come to kill Lacey, I thought. It was the other way around. Lacey had been sent to kill Roxanne.

But even as I came to this conclusion, there was a competing emotion inside me. My mind might be telling me that Lacey was a demon, but my heart still yearned to help her. In two days of talking with her, I have to admit, I had become very attached to her. I had spent the last few days fasting, praying, and trying to find her in order to save her. We had come to love this girl and wanted to do whatever it took to save her. If I felt this way in a few short days, I couldn't imagine how much closer Roxanne felt to her.

Alan and I were still standing at the front counter of the radio station when Roxanne called again. I told her to come over to the church to talk. She said she could leave to drive over in a few minutes. We knew it would take Roxanne about forty-five minutes to make it back to the church from her friend's house. Alan and I called some of the group members who had walked with us through this event and asked them to meet over at the church as well so we could continue this most unusual journey together.

While waiting for Roxanne to arrive, I continued to work on what I would say to her. I was convinced that Lacey was a spirit, and not a friendly one, but rather a demon spirit. She dressed herself as a young victim to elicit sympathy, but she was malignant. The apostle Peter described Satan as a roaring lion: "Be sober, be vigilant; because your adversary the devil walks about like a roaring lion, seeking whom he may devour" (1 Pet. 5:8).

But the apostle Paul also warned us to be on guard: "For Satan himself transforms himself into an angel of light" (2 Cor. 11:14).

What was Roxanne's response going to be when I confronted her with her need to let go of Lacey? When I told her that Lacey was a demon masquerading as a friend? For that matter, what would Lacey's response be? What if she took over Roxanne's body and became violent toward us—or even against Roxanne herself?

I prayed again and again for God to help me. I was trying so hard to say and do the right things, but this was unknown territory for the staff and me. One thing I was sure of: I was not going to give up on someone who needed God's love.

Looking back at this moment today, I would point out that the profession and practice of Christian counseling was relatively new in the early 1980s. Even non-Christian mental health was still a labyrinth of debate, with lots of embarrassment and shame associated with those in need of help. Like its secular counterpart, Christian counseling was a growing movement but not nearly as widespread. There was plenty of discussion in the church about ways Christian theology and modern psychologies were compatible as well as debate about how they were incompatible. I guess there still is, though most pastors and Christian traditions recognize an important place for therapy in ministry. We may not always agree and recognize which problems are primarily spiritual or which are primarily psychological or which need both forgiveness and some form of psychological treatment, but we commonly agree that traditional Christian practices like prayer can be assisted with psychological therapies to bring about growth and healing.

If I had been more aware and educated on certain things at that time, my story about my experiences with Roxanne might have ended right then and there. But I do know that God uses imperfect people with partial and imperfect knowledge and skill to do His work. So I don't look back with apology or regrets. I believe that I emerged from this story with my faith intact and stronger than ever because I was willing to be used.

Roxanne finally knocked on the entrance door of the radio station. I opened the door to let her in. I could see in Roxanne's eyes that she was very uncomfortable and nervous about our second encounter. I brought her into the meeting room where we had done most of our praying and spiritual warfare the night before. Alan and the other group members joined us.

I didn't waste time and asked her directly, "Roxanne, is Lacey inside you?"

Roxanne answered timidly, "I believe she is."

"Roxanne, you know as a child of God you can't have a spirit that is not from God living inside you, don't you?"

She put her head down and wouldn't answer.

"Lacey isn't from God, is she?"

Still no answer.

I spoke as gently and softly as I could. I told Roxanne that if Lacey was inside her, she needed to pray and let go of her and command her to leave in Jesus' name. I told her she now, as a child of God, had the authority to do that, to be free from harmful controlling influences.

I believe this is what Roxanne wanted with all her heart. In a sense, just as Lacey was sent to kill her, she had come to the church the night before to kill Lacey. But it would have been in the form of suicide, and Lacey still would have won. This new way of being rid of a destructive force was alien to her.

Roxanne and I continued to talk about Lacey being inside her. Roxanne began to emotionally pull away from the group and me. She began to grow agitated over the suggestion that she renounce Lacey. She and Lacey had been friends for years, she explained.

"Lacey is the only one who never betrayed me," Roxanne said. "She was always there to help me when the others were mean."

What an anguishing moment. I didn't believe for a second that Lacey had never betrayed Roxanne. As all my thoughts tumbled together, I realized she was not just any demon, but the demon who was orchestrating control over Roxanne's life. But to Roxanne, I was asking her to cast out a teenage girl who was her friend, and upon whom she counted for emotional survival.

Gently, I prodded as much as I felt I could. I suggested to her that it was Lacey who was trying to get Roxanne to commit suicide and kill herself. She didn't see it that way. But after more discussion, Roxanne began to piece things together for herself and see that Lacey had not been a force for good in her life. She began to remember ways that Lacey had hurt her and led her astray. She agreed to pray against Lacey and command her to leave.

As Roxanne began praying I could see her eyes sharpen and then lose focus. I braced myself. I knew that a demon was about to manifest itself inside her again. Next her eyes turned very dark and cold, and as had happened the night before, her face began to contort and change appearance. I could see an anger rising. She looked younger. Then older. Finally, she looked straight into my heart, and I saw hatred and malice. I knew that it wasn't Roxanne looking at me now. It might even be Lacey.

Roxanne's eyes rolled up into the back of her head. But for the moment she didn't stop commanding Lacey to leave. Looking at her, you could see an internal battle bubbling up, ready to explode. Up to this point, I had heard the demons speak with nonhuman voices, men's voices, women's voices, animal sounds, and as multiple voices at once. But something much different happened this time.

Roxanne looked at me and began to speak. It was the

voice of a young, timid, fearful teenager. It was Lacey. After hours on the phone with her, I would never forget her voice.

I had finally found Lacey, but not in the form I expected.

Lacey looked at me and said with a soft, pleading voice, "Bill, it's you. You told me you loved me, that you would fight for me and that you would save me. How can you ask me to leave? Why are you fighting against me? You promised you were different. But now you want to kill me?"

Wow. I was speechless. I had no idea what to say. In my heart I loved Lacey. I had fought for this girl. Her words had a powerful impact on me. Emotionally I agreed with her. How could I be helping to kill the one I was trying to save just a few hours earlier?

Paul could not be more right. I was hearing the sweet words of an angel of light with my own ears.

In the midst of the internal turmoil, I knew that I needed to think with my head and not my heart. There was a new kind of warfare inside me. Much more subtle. Really much more effective. No one is fooled by a roaring lion. But an angel? My heart wanted to reach out to Lacey in love. It took all my willpower to break free from this near spell. I had to tell myself that this was a nasty evil demon masquerading as a helpless little girl trapped inside this woman.

We gathered around Roxanne and laid hands on her as I prayed.

Roxanne interrupted, still speaking in Lacey's voice, and said, "I am not sure if I really want her to go; she is a friend of mine. Lacey helps me."

We were back to square one. I shared again with her that all demons are evil and that Lacey only appeared to be a friend but was actually there to destroy her. I prayed, "Lord, I command Satan in Jesus' name to show himself for who he really is!"

At that moment the sweet little voice turned into a deep, menacing nonhuman voice and yelled, "No!"

Roxanne threw her head back, opened her mouth, and let out a bloodcurdling scream. The demon screamed again and again. Everyone in the room cowered in the presence of evil. Then Lacey left Roxanne and all was quiet. Roxanne just fell to the floor, not moving a muscle. For a fleeting second I was afraid Roxanne had died from the spiritual battle waging inside her.

A few minutes later Roxanne regained consciousness and asked what had happened. She said, "I feel so much different; more free. Is she gone?"

Before we could answer, she exclaimed, "She's gone!"

We looked at one another with joy and the whole group cheered and hugged Roxanne. Tears streamed down her cheeks—and everyone else's in the room.

Two days earlier, I didn't know what a demon sounded like. I had never met someone who claimed to be a witch, much less someone who had been involved in curses, human sacrifice, drinking animal and human blood, and strange and bizarre sexual rituals. I was sure at that point I had certainly seen it all.

But most of all, I felt relief. Now that Lacey was gone, I felt for certain that the battle was won.

Little did I know.

CHAPTER 6

The Houseguest

After spending most of the day with Roxanne, my wife and I were about to leave for home when Roxanne said that she felt she might be in danger if she returned to her friend's home. We asked why. The night before Roxanne had said she would be safe there.

It took her a little time to get it out, but she finally said that the friend she was staying with was heavily involved in the occult with her. If she found out Roxanne had received Christ, she would probably tell others, and that would alert the people who wanted to harm her.

After spending so much time helping Roxanne, that was the last thing we wanted to happen. She needed to be safe and able to establish her new life with Christ. Before I actually knew what I was saying, I blurted out, "You can come home with us!"

My wife's hesitation was palpable. She looked at me, stunned and a bit horrified that I was actually inviting a witch, one who claimed to have been a high satanist priestess, to come home with us.

I will tell you up front it was one of the dumbest moves I have ever made. Everyone reading this knows you consult with your spouse on big decisions that affect your home. Beyond that common courtesy, you simply can't always open your home to the people you are ministering to. There can be a variety of reasons. In this case, there were too many to count off. But I would note that taking home a member of the opposite sex was threatening to my wife of only a few years and, based on appearances alone, not socially appropriate. But the most obvious reason staring me right in the face was my responsibility as a Christian man and husband to provide a home that was a safe place to return to each day. I had invited someone who just hours before was speaking blasphemy and murder.

If you are reading this book to learn what to do correctly in the face of satanic activity, I'll let you in on a secret you've probably already figured out. This book also contains a nice-size list of things not to do. Taking home a person who is or has been demon-possessed is one of them. Incidentally, it took me more than one time to learn this lesson.

The absurdity of what I had done quickly became apparent on the drive home. My wife and I sat in the front seat and Roxanne in the back. She seemed happy to be with us. Much more so than my wife. She did ask us a number of times before we left the church and on the drive what we wanted from her, what she had to do to live with us.

And I could tell from her smile that my wife was pleased to see Roxanne's childlike wonder that we were asking nothing in return from her.

Then Roxanne began to wonder out loud if at some point we were going to force her to have sex with us or anyone else. Talk about awkward and embarrassing. I answered her with a "No" each time she asked that or came up with some other outlandish question. She wondered if she would be our slave and kept in chains in the basement or if we would use her in any other way. I assured her we had no chains and no basement.

I did all I could to remind her of the unconditional love that Jesus Christ has for us and that we can have for one another.

Even if my judgment was far less than perfect, my motives were honorable in inviting Roxanne to be a guest in our home. My only goal was to make sure that she was able to completely separate from the coven without getting hurt so that she could build a wonderful new life in Jesus Christ. Healthy. Happy. Free.

But in addition to her questions about whether we had ulterior motives in bringing her home, Roxanne next started asking about our plans to keep her safe. It was as if we were talking about mundane matters, like what brand of fabric softener we used or our favorite flavor of ice cream. She matter-of-factly stated there was a good chance that members of the coven were not going to like her leaving and would come for her. She said that they killed one member who tried to leave. She wondered out loud if they would try to hurt me for helping her.

My wife just looked at me, her eyes communicating the obvious question: *What have you gotten us into?*

Shortly after arriving at our little duplex and showing Roxanne the guest room where she would be staying, we all went to the living room to talk. I could see that she was getting that look in her eyes again. An internal battle had begun and would soon bubble to the surface.

This can't be happening, I thought. This was not going to happen in our home. Not only had she prayed for salvation, but she had renounced Lacey and asked that Jesus cast Lacey from inside her.

There are a number of ways that Christians look at the conversion of someone who has been demon-possessed or under the influence of a demon. Without getting into the myriad of nuances, most would say there is no room for a demon in or near a Christian's life. But others would say that demons can still have a profound hold on a person, even after they have turned their life over to God through Jesus Christ.

I hadn't given much thought to what position I might hold, but I leaned toward the first view going into this experience. When Christ comes into your life, there is no longer room for anything unclean or evil. But what made Roxanne's situation harder to understand then and now was the fact that, not only were there multiple demons among the voices emanating from her but, there also seemed to be multiple personalities.

I wondered again if someone with a split personality could be saved in one area of their psyche but remain unsaved—and even demon-possessed—in another area.

Without making any strong theological statement, what I believe I saw in my experience with Roxanne at this point and in the days ahead was authentic Christian conversion and numerous authentic exorcisms. But the problem was that demons would be cast out in Jesus' name, only to be allowed—and maybe even invited— back in by some other side of Roxanne.

At minimum I know that a demon can be cast out

of a person and then return. It was Jesus Himself who said:

> When an impure spirit comes out of a person, it goes through arid places seeking rest and does not find it. Then it says, "I will return to the house I left." When it arrives, it finds the house unoccupied, swept clean and put in order. Then it goes and takes with it seven other spirits more wicked than itself, and they go in and live there. And the final condition of that person is worse than the first. That is how it will be with this wicked generation. (Matthew 12:43–45 NIV)

I looked in Roxanne's eyes and saw the battle was now raging, ready to spill out. No sooner did I have that thought than I heard a demon speaking through her. This was happening in my living room. I thought the worst was over? Not even close. Little did I know I hadn't even scratched the surface in this spiritual warfare battle. The demon began to yell, "You will not keep her!"

"Leave in Jesus' name," I shouted back.

To my horror, we were back to square one. The demon just laughed at me.

"I have summoned my followers to come for her," he said. "Roxanne belongs to us; you have no right to her. Let her go!"

There were a number of demons that began to speak through her, each with a different name and personality. As was the case the first two days of being on the phone with Lacey, the demons were trying to intimidate me so I would forget I had God's power inside me. It was working. My wife would not even enter the room but stood in the doorway connecting the living room to the kitchen, a look of incredulity on her face.

So began my first experience with a demon from inside the "safety" of my home. I nodded to my wife, and she knew exactly what I was thinking. She got on the phone and began calling friends from the radio station and church to come to the house and help us pray.

The demon looked at me from Roxanne's body, sitting in the comfort of my living room, promising he would hurt my wife and me. He said a curse over us. He promised to destroy us on every level.

I was shaken to the core but relieved when my wife said friends were on their way over to help us.

Roxanne was a guest in our home. The idea was that this would be a temporary arrangement while we found a ministry organization that could better minister to her and her needs.

It was our first night together, but we spent it praying for her, rebuking demons, casting out demons, and asking the Lord to send His angels to protect us from those who might be coming with the intent to harm us. I was terrified, but there was no way I would be willing to give up in this fight for someone's very soul. I didn't understand the situation, but with my wife and friends at my side to help, I felt from deep within me that the victory would eventually be ours, even if we were fighting Satan himself.

It had been a long, arduous day, and it was getting late. Roxanne seemed to be in a state of relative peace. Friends left to go home one by one. I was so exhausted, I just craved sleep. My wife took Roxanne to her bedroom, which was next to ours. Friends had brought over toiletries and nightwear and a couple of changes of clothes for Roxanne. She seemed pleased as she looked at them through sleepy eyes.

I barely had the energy to brush my teeth before tumbling into bed, my wife right behind. We were nervous with Roxanne next door to us. Would she do something in the middle of the night to harm herself or us? And what about the demons? We prayed a prayer for protection and I stumbled out of bed to make sure Roxanne's door was still shut and to lock the door to our bedroom.

We had no idea what we might have done by putting a witch in our spare bedroom. So despite my fatigue, I double-checked the lock on our bedroom door two more times.

A couple of hours later my wife elbowed me in the ribs. She heard something coming from Roxanne's room. I timidly opened our bedroom door and stood by Roxanne's door, trying to hear if anything was going on. I listened hard and could hear her talking and voices talking back to her. If I wouldn't have had the experience of hearing multiple voices coming from the same person over the past few days, I would have sworn there was a group of four or five people in the room holding a conversation.

She kept talking back and forth with what seemed like several different people, but she was the only one in the room. Some of the voices were normal and others were creepy; most were female, but some were male. I couldn't hear everything clearly, but some seemed to be human voices and others the voices of spirits. What was strikingly different from the voices I had heard coming out of her before was that now there was no anger or cursing. It was almost like listening to a group of good friends carrying on a conversation.

So what was I supposed to do? Barge in and confront Roxanne and do more battle with the demons? I was exhausted. Roxanne was a guest in our home. Maybe I was rationalizing, but I realized there was no way I was going to open her bedroom door. I figured this was one meeting I was not invited to, so I crept back down the hall and got back in bed with my wife and tried to sleep.

As my head hit the pillow I wondered again, *What have I done? What have I brought into our home?* Had I gone crazy? Was all that had been happening to me in the last few days real?

CHAPTER 7

Demons Go to Church

The night was long and fitful, filled with much tossing and turning, drifting off into a restless sleep and then waking up with a start, eyes wide open, making sure nothing but my wife and I were in the room, making sure we were safe. It's hard to sleep when there is a meeting of evil spirits in your spare bedroom.

The alarm sounded both too quickly and not soon enough. It was Sunday morning. We got up and knocked on Roxanne's door to tell her it was time to get ready for church. We wondered if she would put up a fight about having to go to church with us, but to our pleasant surprise, she rose quickly and enthusiastically answered, "Okay."

She got ready fast and walked to the kitchen to sit down beside me for breakfast. With a sparkle in her eye, she told me that she had never attended church. Later, as we were eating, she asked me again what kind of sacrifices took place at our church, human or animal? I never ceased to be amazed at how she could ask the most outrageous questions with a seemingly normal tone and expression. The lines seemed to be coming from a bad script or a bad movie. I simply told her that just as I had explained there would be no sacrifices in our home, neither would any sacrifices occur at our church this week or any other week, human or otherwise.

She next wanted to know if we would drink any blood during the service. I almost laughed as I wondered if this was the time to tell her about Communion and explain the meaning of the elements.

But any levity was quickly replaced by just how serious all this was to her. Behind her questions, she was really asking if she was going to be hurt. While walking to the car you could see by Roxanne's dark eyes the demons were not happy. I wondered what would happen if we had another demonic episode in the car on the drive to church. As much as she thrashed around, I might not be able to keep control of the car.

But we pulled out of the neighborhood and made it onto the highway ramp without incident. I would look in the rearview mirror to see how she was doing, and from time to time her eyes would go blank. My wife and I looked at each other as we neared the church. But there wasn't the escalation of movement and facial contortions that signaled the demons would soon be controlling her.

Then Roxanne growled at us. It wasn't the voice of a demon. It was her voice, not imitating but making the sound of a wild animal.

As we pulled into the parking lot, I worried about what might actually happen during the church service. As I pushed the gearshift forward into Park, I could see Roxanne was getting more and more nervous. But I didn't sense the onset and onslaught of a demonic episode. We walked up the steps to the front door and went inside to the sanctuary and sat down. I thought about what we called our worship center: the *sanctuary*. I'm not sure when or how the church began calling this special place a sanctuary—in the Old Testament I know there were cities of sanctuary—but however it was first used, the word itself was calming and reassuring to me.

The worship service began and everything seemed to be going along fine. Roxanne seemed to enjoy the singing and I noticed she had a nice voice. But when the pastor began to preach, I could hear Roxanne growl at some of the things being taught. It was soft and so only a few people in our immediate area looked over our way, trying to figure out who was making the noise. Then I heard the voice of a demon. Again, it was in the softest of voices, not the shrieking and screaming tones we had grown accustomed to. But it was loud enough that a few more people in our area seemed to be looking around, trying to find out who was talking and making noises when the pastor was preaching.

I clearly heard one demon say, "____ this; we have to get her out of here."

Red-faced, I looked around. I wondered if anyone else could make out what the demons were actually saying. My breathing was shallow and I wondered what in the world would happen next. It's funny how the mind works. Not only was I afraid for myself and others that a demon was going to interrupt the church service and unleash his rage, but I was also feeling incredibly embarrassed that those around us might hear the demon using profanity.

When speaking to Peter, Jesus said to him: "I also say to you that you are Peter, and on this rock I will build My church, and the gates of Hades shall not prevail against it" (Matt. 16:18).

Just as I had discovered the evening before that my

home was not a fortress against the presence of demons, I now learned that church walls weren't demon-proof either. The armies of hell could not defeat the church because the church is something much more than brick-and-mortar walls. But apparently demons can attend church if invited by the right person. Our sanctuary didn't feel like a sanctuary to me at that moment.

The same demon spoke again, apparently directly to me: "You'll pay for doing this to us."

Out of all the Sundays for Roxanne to make her first ever visit to church, it had to be Communion Sunday. I thought to myself, *This is not going to go over well*, and it didn't. The pastor said we were drinking Christ's blood and eating His body when we partook of the juice and cracker given to each of us. He did make brief mention that the elements were only representative of Christ's flesh and blood, our church's view of the sacraments. I don't think Roxanne heard that part, because she freaked out when she heard we would drink blood and eat flesh. Her eyes went wide. She looked from me to my wife and back again. She wiggled in her seat like it was on fire. It took me a few minutes to get her to calm down as I whispered to her what Holy Communion actually meant; that the bread and juice were *symbolic* of flesh and blood.

We made it through the church service and ducked out quickly to head home. We were too tired to prepare a meal, so we decided to stop on the way home for burgers. As we worked our way through the crowd and out the door, we invited a couple of friends to join us who had been involved in the whole Roxanne ordeal the past few days. I was relieved to have the emotional and spiritual support of others.

But on the way to the restaurant Roxanne began to grow agitated again, saying, "They are coming to get me. I can feel it; they are getting close."

I was trying not to look nervous, but my eyes darted to other cars near us to make sure someone wasn't closing in on us. My knees were knocking again, which made keeping the speed consistent a tough task.

We got to the restaurant unharmed, sat down at a table large enough to seat seven of us, and made several attempts to include Roxanne in some small talk to lower her stress level. She had gone from looking worried to looking terrified.

Unfortunately, I made matters worse rather than better. I asked our friends if they knew that a mutual friend of ours was now pregnant. But I worded it all wrong, saying, "She has a baby in the oven."

Roxanne began to grow hysterical as she pointed a finger at me and accused, "You guys do that? How could you kill babies? I thought you said you were different!"

I was taken aback until I realized what I had said. I began to explain that "in the oven" was just a figure of speech. She calmed down. Then, not making eye contact with anyone, she said that she had seen a number of babies sacrificed over the years in many different ways.

Not surprisingly, lunch ended up being a rather heavy emotional experience as Roxanne told us about the more extreme and bizarre activities of satanic witchcraft. I've learned since then that there is a wide variety of witchcraft groups—from New Age to feminist to ecologically based and combined movements—and most do not consider themselves to be evil or violent. I'm not going to sort out definitions of evil here, but suffice it to say that what she described had to be the most virulent, hard-core branch of witchcraft in existence.

She told us again how young girls were raised in covens so they could serve as breeders. That's how she got started in her coven. She spoke of many things in nonemotional, matter-of-fact tones, but not on this topic. Apparently, her God-given maternal instinct cut through any and all evil that inhabited her and she felt incredible sorrow over the loss of even one baby.

She told of eating real flesh and drinking warm blood during communion in the coven.

She told us that many high-level officials in our government are part of covens, and that witches come from every stratum of society, but perhaps more from the wealthy class than the middle and poorer classes.

I will say that as she shared all this, it was confusing to look at Roxanne. I still thought of her as a helpless, timid young teen from all my talks with Lacey. Not as a thirty-something woman and certainly not as a major player in a coven. But she was speaking with confidence and what seemed to be real knowledge.

Could this same person be both a leader and a victim? Was Roxanne not only someone who had been terribly abused but someone who directed the abuse of others?

She told us that covens were asked to pray over certain music CDs, horror flicks, and other media dealing with dark subjects before they were released. Roxanne said they specifically prayed that spirits would go with every CD and that demons would leave with those who went to see the horror movies. Roxanne said she and others from her coven put curses on people who opposed them and that some of the curses could actually kill a person. Most commonly, curses dealt with relationships. She said the breakup of Christian marriages had always been a high priority.

She said that some witches were able to "soul travel," leaving their bodies and passing through space to instantly be in other parts of the world, much as a voice being transmitted from one phone to another across the globe.

If even a small portion of what Roxanne was sharing was true, it was evident that the power of satanic covens was enormous and alarming.

And I, Bill Scott, was going to go up against this? I already had a demon say that he was putting a curse on me. Was I crazy?

In the days ahead I think many in my church began to suspect just that, including those in leadership. It's not that people doubted we had faced and experienced something mysterious and evil—and undoubtedly satanic, but I don't think people wanted to hear about our troubles and face it themselves, so it was easier to ignore.

In his classic work *The Screwtape Letters,* C. S. Lewis wrote:

> There are two equal and opposite errors into which our race can fall about the devils. One is to disbelieve in their existence. The other is to believe, and to feel an excessive and unhealthy interest in them. They themselves are equally pleased by both errors and hail a materialist or magician with the same delight.[1]

I'm sure some suspected that in the days ahead I developed an excess interest in demons and satanic witchcraft.

I won't argue any of those points. I certainly agree my life would have been easier had I walked away from Roxanne and all the baggage she brought into our home and our lives.

But I was in a dilemma. Roxanne. How could I simply leave this person in need to face things all alone? A person whose eternal soul and destiny hung in the balance of my willingness to help?

It was time to say our good-byes and head home. Roxanne was looking all over the inside and outside of the restaurant because she was certain that the other witches and warlocks were coming for her. This put me back on guard. Could she be right?

We walked out the front door and into the parking lot, where one of the weirdest things I've ever witnessed happened.

Halfway to the car, black hawks came out of nowhere and began to circle us. Before I knew what was happening, the black hawks had landed and formed a circle around us. There we stood in a suburban parking lot, completely surrounded by birds of prey glaring at us.

"They are here," Roxanne said in a low, quavering voice. "My friends are inside the birds. They found me."

Her friends the demons? It would have helped my state of mind had she not referred to them as her friends.

I grabbed my wife by an elbow with one hand and Roxanne's elbow with the other. I was going to get us out of here. I let out what was supposed to be a menacing yell and pulled the ladies along as I ran for the car. The birds jumped back enough to give us a narrow path to the car. I pushed the women inside on their side of the car and slammed both doors shut. The birds had gathered there in a small flock and glared at me. I waved my arms and yelled again as I ran around to my side of the car. They barely moved this time, but nothing touched me as I made it inside the car safely.

I started the engine and pulled out of the parking lot, barely glancing around. Fortunately, traffic wasn't heavy. I just wanted to get us away from those beady black eyes maliciously staring at us.

We drove home in silence.

Like so many other events that occurred from the moment Lacey called my radio-station phone line—from the day Satan called—I cannot be certain what happened. Were there witches inside the birds? I can't prove it, but based on timing and everything else that had occurred, I believe there were. I had no other explanation than what Roxanne said: Witches traveled in the bodies of birds. I became paranoid, imagining that I was constantly being followed by and watched by birds, but nothing this dramatic ever happened again.

As we drove to the house I again felt deeply exhausted. It had been four long, intense, terrifying days with bizarre, scary, amazing things happening at every turn. As we walked through the door at home, all I hoped for was a Sunday afternoon nap. Apparently I was hoping for way too much.

Roxanne wanted to talk about what she was experiencing. And she was having a hard time understanding God's unconditional love—along with ours. Why would anyone help her and not demand something in return? We spent the next few hours talking with her and answering her questions the best we could. Despite the topics covered, it was a relatively uneventful conversation, which at this point was truly a refreshing change. After talking to Roxanne, we nervously walked back to our room to take a nap.

Sunday evening came, and though my wife and I almost always went to the evening service, for some reason—maybe it was just fatigue—I stayed home with Roxanne and a friend who lived close by while my wife drove to the church alone. Soon, maybe because my wife was gone or she was uncomfortable with someone present she hadn't met before, Roxanne started to become agitated. Her eyes turned very cold and dark. I thought of the birds from earlier in the afternoon.

I had warned my friend about what had been happening. I think he was curious enough to agree to come over. But I don't think he was prepared for what happened next.

A demon started speaking out of Roxanne.

"Roxanne will die for her decision to leave us," the demon said.

My friend and I prayed for her and rebuked the demon.

Other demons joined him in speaking against us. But this time they introduced themselves by name.

I can't remember the exact names the demons called themselves—and even if I could, I'm not sure I could spell them—but I am convinced they were spoken to intimidate and terrify my friend and me.

The apostle John tells us: "There is no fear in love; but perfect love casts out fear, because fear involves torment. But he who fears has not been made perfect in love" (1 John 4:18).

It is interesting that fear and love are connected that

way. What I had learned and was learning anew with each encounter was the way demons used fear to beat you—beat me—before the fight had even begun.

I am in no way discounting how powerful these entities were, but I had the love of God inside me, and therefore the only way the demons could defeat me was if I didn't use what had been given to me.

I would tell anyone reading this book who feels defeated by fear to turn to God and ask Him to help you experience the full measure of His love. You'll be amazed at how that realization does cast out fear.

Roxanne's body began to twist into unusual positions as she sat on the sofa with the demons speaking from her. She growled with real animal sounds and even spit at us.

I wondered, not for the first or last time, why I couldn't put her out of my house and life. But even as I asked myself the question, I already knew the answer: Abandoning her was the same as handing her over to Satan; we had a battle to win. I didn't ask for it. But God had given it to me.

So I went toe-to-toe with those demons in Jesus' name. I was smart enough not to do anything in my own strength or name. I didn't have all the information I needed for this battle, but I knew it had to be fought in Jesus' name and that I was not to take credit for anything.

We battled on. Roxanne was knocked off the sofa onto the floor. We didn't see anything attack her, but from the way her body jerked forward, something had hit her and hit her hard. I began to plead the blood of Jesus over Roxanne so she would not be hurt. Then my friend nudged me and pointed at her hands. He had noticed that she had one fist closed and something was in it. At the same time the demon kept saying, "I am going to kill her; I am going to kill her. She is mine, and I am going to kill her."

Something was very wrong. We pried open Roxanne's fist so we could see what was in her hand. Roxanne had a handful of razor blades.

How did she get these? She hadn't left the sofa but had been with us the whole time. I was sure we didn't have regular razor blades in our house.

"I know what you're thinking," the demon said with a laugh. "I brought them myself so we could finish the job!"

Was it possible for spirits to carry physical things? Just when I thought things couldn't get stranger, it now seemed that demons were able to cause the people they possessed to carry weapons that could harm them.

This fight went on for about three hours. We prayed with Roxanne; we read Scripture to her; we had praise and worship music playing on the stereo.

When my wife returned from church I knew we needed to talk. We were not qualified to continue helping Roxanne. We could not fight demons inside our own home.

But I was still not going to give up. I knew that the number one priority was to look for a person or ministry that was qualified to work with Roxanne.

There would be five more days of this torment before I found what we thought was the answer to helping Roxanne.

How wrong I was. Again.

CHAPTER 8

The Journey Begins

As I look back at this point in the story and think about my experience, I'm as amazed as you are. Before the day Satan called, did I believe there was evil in the world? Of course I did. But supernatural evil with real demons? I know I at least intellectually believed in a real Satan, but probably not to a degree that I gave him or his works any thought or worry. Even as a kid I really wasn't afraid of the dark.

Did I ever think that I would meet evil face-to-face? I was a committed Christian, and I think I anticipated confronting some forms of evil on moral issues—maybe in areas like the pro-life movement or decency standards in music and other media.

But did I ever think I would meet evil personified in a person and the spirits that inhabited her? I wouldn't have dreamed of talking to a demon on the phone. I never thought I'd meet a witch, much less bring one home.

You might be wondering, "Bill, how did you know it was a demon on the phone?" I could list all of the things I saw and experienced—from a strange gathering of birds that surrounded me outside a restaurant to someone on a phone line knowing when people were entering and leaving a room—but my fundamental response would be and is still quite simple: I knew a demon was on the phone because the voice was not human.

I've already cataloged for you my physical responses to the voice, from every hair on my body standing straight up to heaviness of breathing and light-headedness. I also mentioned that on more than one occasion the temperature in the room dropped so quickly I felt like I was in a meat locker when the demon was speaking.

For years I kept a recording of some of my conversations with this demon. For those who laughed at me and refused to believe it was a demon—and if it had been someone else telling me the story, I might have been a scoffer, too—I would invite them to hear the tape and decide for themselves if (a) this was a human voice and (b) if they thought it was the voice of a demon. I would put the tape in the machine and hit Play. Usually within seconds they would beg me to turn the tape off. They knew that it was a demon, that it was not a human voice. I finally burned the tapes. I didn't want to keep anything that evil in my presence.

During the writing of this book I made a few references to this time in my life on my Facebook page. A good friend who worked at the same radio station as I did during this ordeal gave me a call and said they were going through archives and thought they might still have a few recordings of our talks with Lacey and the demons. He asked me if I wanted him to keep them or toss them if he found them. After some internal debate I said yes, keep them—though I hope to never listen to them again.

Another friend of mine mentioned that when he was in Alaska, he met a nine-year-old Inuit boy who was demon-possessed. This surprised me. I wasn't sure he believed in that kind of thing. He told me something similar to what I experienced: "You know the voices you are hearing are not human when every hair on your body stands on end. You know for sure it's a demon speaking—whether you can prove it or not."

My friend told me this boy would talk with strange voices, growl like a wild animal—not like a boy imitating a wild animal but a wild animal—and become violent. At one point he watched the boy dig a tooth out of his mouth with just his fingers—and smile through the blood. Peter said this wasn't a baby tooth that was barely hanging on and ready to fall out. What made our conversation so interesting was that, like me, my friend is the most unlikely person to have come face-to-face with some form of supernatural activity and satanic possession based on any predisposition of upbringing or personality. I believe he is a person of faith, and I know he attends a local church fellowship on occasion. But his church tradition would be much more skeptical of supernatural phenomenon than the small independent church I grew up in, which had plenty of reservations of its own.

At this point in my experience with Roxanne, I was hoping that the worst was over. I was not able to completely comprehend all I had seen and heard so far. I was in a state of continuous fear; my faith had been rocked, and my wife and I were divided on what we should do next to help this woman. But I was certain that I did not want to stop fighting the fight for her. To give up at this point would be to admit Satan had won, which was something I just couldn't do. I was in my twenties, full of passion, and more than a little stubborn, so losing this battle wasn't an option for me. I knew if we could help Roxanne more fully tap into God's power, we would defeat Satan. But to be honest, if I had known this was barely the beginning, I probably would have walked away. Not based on what the wise Christian thing was to do, but more because of a sense of discouragement and hopelessness.

I've already told you that the biggest mistake I made was inviting Roxanne into my home without consulting with my wife. I've also told you that one of the priorities of the coven that Roxanne was a member of was the breakup of Christian marriages. There are many notes of victory throughout this book, and the ending is a beautiful testament to God's never-ending love and mercy for Roxanne and all of us. But I must confess, there would be many defeats and casualties in this battle for Roxanne, including my own marriage and the marriages of others who were in the midst of the fight before and after Roxanne entered my life and my wife's life.

Can I put the blame for my marital failure on Roxanne? Of course not. But I can say without any doubt that if you are ever faced with a difficult spiritual battle and have a choice of whether to engage or walk away, please walk away if you are not of one heart and mind with those who must walk the journey with you.

There is a famous Abraham Lincoln quote with which most of us are familiar: "A house divided against itself cannot stand."

But the inspiration behind the quote originated in the words of Jesus. This is what He said:

One was brought to Him who was demon-possessed, blind and mute; and He healed him, so that the blind and mute man both spoke and saw. And all the multitudes were amazed and said, "Could this be the Son of David?" Now when the Pharisees heard it they said, "This fellow does not cast out demons except by Beelzebub, the ruler of the demons."

But Jesus knew their thoughts, and said to them: "Every kingdom divided against itself is brought to desolation, and every city or house divided against itself will not stand." (Matthew 12:22–25)

There are many lessons to be learned from my story, but one of the most vital is the importance of oneness within your family.

CHAPTER 9

An Answer to Prayer

Several days passed, and each day was similar to the one before. My wife and I had now spent a week fighting demons and staving off Roxanne's suicide attempts, which were daily occurrences. Now there were even voices of demons that could be heard throughout my house that didn't come from Roxanne. Some were angry; others sounded as if they were in normal conversation. They could have been talking about the weather or a sale at the mall. There were physical manifestations of the demons. The closet door in my short hallway from the living room to the bedrooms opened and shut on its own. When I heard this I would quickly take a look around the corner from the living room or outside my bedroom door to see if it was Roxanne. No one was ever there.

The light in the hall bathroom and one of the lights in the kitchen turned on and off during the night. My wife and I would question Roxanne and then each other about leaving lights on, but as with the door opening and shutting, it was obvious this was happening independent of the three of us.

Bill Scott, a grown man, was now sleeping with his bedroom light on. If I still had my childhood teddy bear, he would have joined us in bed each night.

If not for that small group of friends who also didn't want to give up on Roxanne, we would never have made it through that first week. A week doesn't sound very long, but to us it felt like a lifetime, a never-ending nightmare.

It was obvious we needed outside assistance in order to get Roxanne the help she needed. We simply couldn't monitor her 24/7 to keep her safe from injuring or killing herself. We also needed a very specific kind of help to get rid of the evil forces running amok in our house.

I quickly discovered you can't call most of your local churches to ask for help with a demon-possessed young woman. Churches have youth pastors and music leaders, but not many have a "minister of exorcism." Seriously, I believe Satan does most of his work through the natural inclination toward evil of "fallen man" and doesn't commonly manifest himself through supernatural phenomena. I still believe that. So not surprisingly, most churches don't know how to deal with a situation like Roxanne's and are not equipped for a long-term relationship with someone like her. If someone called your church, who would be responsible for dealing with a demon-possessed person, and over an extended period of time?

After spending hours on the phone and praying for God to show us who would help us in this new season of Roxanne's life, we came across a ministry organization that handled severely emotionally and behaviorally troubled teenagers and young adults. Even though she was in her thirties and outside their ministry focus, I was able to set up an interview for Roxanne to see if they would take her in as a special case. Each person accepted into the program needed a sponsor to pay for their stay. We weren't making much money and couldn't afford to pay what was a very modest fee, but the local director could tell from our calls we were desperate and was open to helping us. He said he would trust God to provide the money.

The three of us drove out to the countryside in order to visit the campus. It wasn't terribly impressive, just a couple of old homes in the middle of nowhere, but from my phone conversations, I sensed these folks were highly competent and caring—and much better equipped to help Roxanne than my wife and I were. We left Roxanne in the waiting area and sat down with the director in his office, where we shared as much of Roxanne's story as we knew. I told the man a few times, "She has demons." I don't think he heard me or totally believed me, so every few minutes I would repeat that she had demons. He probably thought I was crazy or at least exaggerating. Having worked with many troubled young people, I think he suspected that what I was calling demon possession was really a mental or psychological disorder.

Roxanne was then brought in to meet with the director and an assistant. My wife and I were allowed to stay but were told that we weren't to make comments. Roxanne was eager and cooperative. The director told her the program lasted for nine months. He stressed that, most important, if she was going to be helped, she had to want the help. Roxanne was told they had a long waiting list, but they were willing to move her to the front if she wanted to come. She said that she did. I was singing hallelujah and rejoicing inside. I didn't think things could go any better.

The interview was very intense, but Roxanne was pleasant and agreeable at each step of the discussion, even when she was told the rules. She barely blinked an eye when they said, "No music, daily classes, very strict visitation guidelines; and you can never leave the property without permission. If you ever decide to leave, keep walking and we will send your belongings to you."

This was a onetime, one-chance deal. They explained there were too many people who wanted to be in the program for them to spend time with anyone who was not serious about getting help.

There were additional meetings that didn't include us, which made me nervous that something might happen to scuttle this opportunity, but after a long interview process, the director let me know Roxanne was accepted into the program.

I was amazed and so grateful. Roxanne was going to get the help she needed. Our life was going to get back to normal. What an answer to prayer! I believe that my heart skipped a number of beats in relief and excitement. Roxanne would be admitted into the program the next day.

The three of us returned home then. That night was no different. Demons spoke through Roxanne. She had again mysteriously managed to get her hands on razor blades. But we prayed with her and over her all night, and she was calm and unharmed in the morning. I don't believe she remembered anything about the night before.

We drove Roxanne back to the campus to officially enroll her in the program. She had a very old car that she could have used to get there, but we figured it would be best if we left it in our driveway. We didn't want to

take any chances of making it easy for her to leave once
we got her there. I'll never forget the drive. She was no
longer pleasant and agreeable.

The demons were angry and vocal and one kept saying
to us, "The witches will find her; she'll escape; you cannot hide her there."

These words were accompanied by growling noises
and sometimes Roxanne as herself, agitated and wondering where we were taking her. I could handle it this
time, because in just a few more miles Roxanne would
no longer be our problem. I felt we had done our part.
We had fought as hard as we could in the battle for Roxanne's soul, and now we were about to be free.

We pulled up to one of the center's homes and I took
Roxanne into the director's office. Two ladies in charge
of the day-to-day care were there. It was the first time
they had met Roxanne. We told them her story in detail,
including accounts of drug abuse, sexual promiscuity and
abuse, satanic ritual abuse, the practice of witchcraft, and
all the other details we had learned over the last week.
I shared several times that she had demons—and, once
again, it seemed that my opinion was ignored.

I think many well-intentioned but frustrated Christians
have accused someone who is difficult of having demons
to explain the deviant behavior. These ladies, both from
tough backgrounds and not timid or likely to be intimi-
dated in any way, listened to me politely, but apparently
they had heard this diagnosis before. Even as we spoke
I was relieved to be leaving Roxanne there, but worried.
About them. I wanted to somehow warn them that they
probably hadn't dealt with anyone quite like Roxanne.

This would be a battle unlike anything they had ever

encountered. On the drive over the demons had made it clear they did not want Roxanne at this place that lifted up the name of Jesus as the answer to life's problems.

While I was there, I had a chance to talk with a few of the teens and young adults who were in the program. Some had been drug dealers, others prostitutes, and still others thieves. Most had been in fights and had the scars to prove it. Most had dropped out of high school. Many had been convicted of a crime and were sent to the program instead of jail as a last-chance measure by the sentencing judge. To say these were some pretty rough characters would be an understatement.

I did notice that no one else I met mentioned witch-craft as part of their former life, so I concluded that Roxanne was probably the only witch there.

The program boasted a 90 percent success rate. How do you quantify that kind of success? I didn't know, but I had no doubt that the program was effective. I was so impressed with the leaders—even if they didn't seem to take me seriously when I talked about demons. All the leaders had spent time on the streets with drugs and other addictions, and they had made it through the program themselves. They knew firsthand what the kids they were working with had experienced. They were visible success stories. Perhaps Roxanne would be the next big break-through for this organization. I knew we had enrolled her in the right place.

A couple of the leaders took my wife and me for a tour around the campus. The buildings were old and had no air-conditioning. We lived in a region of the country where summers were so hot you could literally fry an egg on the sidewalk. I asked them why there was no air-conditioning.

They said that they purposefully made conditions hard on those who were in the program. They did not want the time there to be easy, but wanted the participants to have to pay a price to get well so it would mean more to them. The young people needed to understand what had brought them to this place in their lives—literally and figuratively— and feel that they had accomplished something great when they graduated. It sounded a little like a Christian boot camp run by military officers who had become ministers, but my wife and I were impressed they had thought things through so meticulously. Bottom line, they had a track record of getting people off the street and watching them become responsible, contributing members of church and society.

Before leaving I sat down with the director and one of the "home mothers," this time with Roxanne not present. Once again I shared everything I knew. I think they were more than tired of hearing me repeat myself, but I still felt it necessary to walk through the details one more time. I reminded them that Roxanne had drunk human and animal blood during satanic rituals. She had seen and been a part of human sacrifices. She had been a breeder in a coven and offered up her babies for sacrifices. She was one of the few people who had successfully left the coven—and Roxanne was still worried she would be found and killed. I wanted the staff to know beyond a shadow of a doubt what they were in for. They were the ones who would be investing their time in her for the next nine to twelve months.

I then told them in minute detail of my personal experiences since the first day "Lacey" phoned my call-in line. They didn't think I was lying. I think they just felt I was someone who saw supernatural acts of Satan in events that could have a different explanation.

When it was time to go, my wife and I at least knew that we had done our very best to warn the staff about what they might face.

I was told it would be a month before we could visit Roxanne, so we could look forward to at least a thirty-day break from contact with her. I know that sounds cold, but we were in desperate need of getting our lives back to some semblance of order. We had jobs and ministries that had been neglected. Our home had been the playground of demons. We were not heartless. We were committed to praying every day for Roxanne's complete spiritual deliverance and emotional healing. But we needed the demons and all the evil we had heard and seen to be behind us for our own spiritual sakes.

We stayed close to Roxanne as long as we were allowed. We knew it would be awhile before we saw her again and wanted to assure her of our love and prayers. My wife had not asked for Roxanne to be in our home, but she, too, felt very sad and hugged her tightly before we drove off.

We were aware that the program was struggling financially and was making a big sacrifice to take Roxanne in—they could have put her at the back of the list and taken another person who had a paying sponsor—so before heading home, we drove to a nearby town and bought some food, toilet paper, and other supplies they needed. We didn't have a lot of money, but what we did have we wanted to share with these folks who had so graciously and sacrificially agreed to help Roxanne.

I told the leaders that I would help any chance I got

and would try to get the radio station I worked for be-hind the program to help them raise support. Perhaps we could do remote broadcasts and have our listeners deliver food or other essential items that were needed. These people were my knights in shining armor at this point. Where else could Roxanne go? Of all the churches and ministries we had contacted, this was the only one that agreed to help Roxanne.

As we finally drove away, my wife and I talked about the last week and the days ahead. We felt good about leaving Roxanne with these folks. My wife was never in favor of bringing a witch into our home, and she had been right. But she wasn't complaining or blaming me—she had a big heart for ministry as well. As the miles ticked by, we felt a peace that our ordeal with Roxanne was over and we would no longer have to deal with the demons and witches and warlocks that swirled around her life.

Most of all, we were excited that our house would be home again. Safe. Blessedly peaceful and quiet.

The Haunted House

We finally got home, and it was the first time in a week that our house was quiet, with nobody to watch, nobody to pray over, and no demons growling, spitting, cursing, blaspheming, and screeching in our living room. It was nice not to have to figure out who would be on suicide watch should things head in that direction with Roxanne. There was no need to be scared; we were safe, and things were back to normal once again.

My wife and I had dinner, watched some TV, and just enjoyed a laid-back evening. We did what we could. Roxanne was in good hands. Finally it was time to go to bed. I was exhausted and hoped I could get a full night's sleep for the first time in more than a week.

I lay in bed and watched a little more TV before turning the lights out. I lay there, once again thinking about everything I had seen, heard, and experienced. Just before drifting off, I was suddenly wide awake. I could feel a presence in my house. An evil presence. What was going on? Roxanne was gone, wasn't she?

My first thought was that I was just scared because of the things I had seen and my imagination was playing tricks on me. I didn't want fear to get a foothold, so I tried to ignore what I was feeling. But the more I tried, the stronger the feeling became. The more I told myself not to think about it, the more I was aware of something uninvited in the house. It was getting hard to breathe. Thoughts were racing through my head. How could this be? The battle was supposed to be over. Roxanne was no longer here. What could be causing this? What was it? Was it a demon or a trace of a demon?

I continued to lie in my bed, trying to ignore the evil presence in the room. Then it happened. The bathroom light turned on, all by itself. The click of the switch was crystal clear.

This wasn't the first time our lights had turned on and off by themselves. It had happened when Roxanne was there. But now it really took me by surprise with Roxanne physically gone. My heart started to pound. I wondered for a second if I might be having a heart attack. I could actually hear my heart beating. The sense of dread was overpowering.

During this time my wife had said nothing, but now she pushed herself up to a sitting position in the bed and looked at me with wide eyes. There was a pleading look in her expression. It was obvious she was terrified. I felt helpless to do anything about it. I was just as afraid as she was.

She asked me to go turn out the light. I wish I could tell you I bounded out of bed and commanded the forces of evil in God's name to leave once and for all...right now!

But what I said was, "No way; if they want it on, it can stay on all night long."

It did. We pulled the covers up over us as high as we could and still breathe.

We didn't get a lot of sleep that night. The evil presence just lingered in the air. Finally morning arrived and I was never so glad to see daylight in my life. Our emotions had calmed down, and neither of us could feel a foreign presence any longer, evil or otherwise. But why were we still having problems? Roxanne was miles away.

My hope was that what we experienced was just a onetime aberration—strange and scary—but just the last vibrations of Roxanne's time as our houseguest.

At the studio I told what happened that night to some of my coworkers and asked them to pray for us. My boss, James, had everyone gather around me and pray. I was very appreciative, not only of the prayer itself, but also of the care and encouragement of friends.

I felt that I could now tackle my first post-Roxanne day back at work without fear and distraction. And my day did go great and time sped by. No demons on the request line. No small crowd gathered around me in the studio to uphold me in prayer—as nice as that was, it had still been fatiguing. I walked out the door to hop in my car for the drive home with a spring in my step and a sense of energy I hadn't felt for more than a week.

It was night two without Roxanne. Our evening started uneventful and quiet. We spent some time praying for Roxanne. Then I felt a strong impression to check under the bed in our guest room where Roxanne had stayed. I do not know why, but I ignored it.

Maybe I was really afraid to admit to my wife and myself just how frightened I really was. So I did nothing.

You've probably heard the quote "The only thing we have to fear is fear itself." Franklin D. Roosevelt said this in his first inaugural address. Here is the complete sentence:

> So, first of all, let me assert my firm belief that the only thing we have to fear is fear itself—nameless, unreasoning, unjustified terror which paralyzes needed efforts to convert retreat into advance.

The context of FDR's speech was the Great Depression. I think I was feeling my own version of the great personal depression at the moment. I could relate too well with Roosevelt's words; terror had paralyzed my "needed efforts to convert retreat into advance."

Sometime that evening I once again felt that inner voice telling me to check under the bed Roxanne had slept in. I continued to ignore it because I thought I was just scared and confused. I was sure that if I did nothing the feeling would eventually go away.

Soon it was time to go to bed. I was trying to look and feel brave in front of my wife, but I was actually wondering if our battle with demons was really over. What if there was a repeat of last night?

I wasn't tired, but I went to bed at my normal time. I turned off the lights and got under the covers. Almost immediately I began to feel an evil presence again. Unlike the previous night's experience, this time I couldn't rationalize the impression away or attribute the feeling to an overactive imagination. Suddenly our guest bedroom door slammed shut! My wife was startled and scared as she looked to me for comfort. My heart was pounding away, and I just lay there, shaking my head back and forth as if to say, "No! No! No!"

I couldn't believe it. There was no doubt in my mind that my house was haunted. The bathroom light turned on again and there were noises coming from throughout the house: footsteps, a hinge squeaking, voices in conversation, breathing, and some bumping sounds. I wanted to be brave but wasn't able to force myself to get out of bed. I knew for a fact my wife and I were the only ones in the house, at least the only flesh-and-blood humans in the house. I had done my nightly routine of checking to make sure all doors and windows were securely shut and locked.

It was just the two of us, but we weren't alone. I could still feel that heavy evil presence, even stronger than the night before. Events of the past week should have been diminishing. Instead, they seemed to be increasing in ever more bizarre ways.

We slept fitfully off and on, hearing sounds most of the night, never once leaving the safety of our bed. The first rays of morning light felt like a blessing from God. The house seemed to return to normal during daylight hours.

I went to work and asked people to keep praying for us. I didn't care what others thought of me at this point. I just blurted out, "Our house is haunted." A few of our friends said they would come over and pray for us and pray over the house and anoint it with oil. Outside Old Testament stories, I had never really heard of anointing anything with oil—I later found out that in many Christian traditions this was a common practice, especially for healing and commissioning services. I thought it sounded like a wonderful idea.

As soon as I arrived home from work I told my wife that a few friends would be coming over after dinner to

pray over and anoint our home to banish the evil presence. We had been anxiously waiting for our friends to
arrive, and were relieved to hear the doorbell ring. Our
friends were ready to offer a prayer of blessing and protection over our home. One of the men carried a small
vile of oil to anoint the doors and each room of the
house. The oil is a symbol of the presence of the Holy
Spirit.

We joined hands for a prayer of commitment and then
walked together through each room, marking the top of
the doorways with a cross of oil and commanding any
and all evil to leave our home. There were a few times
when we would pray and instantly feel the temperature
in the room lower. Every hair on my head would stand
on end as we prayed, and I wasn't the only one to feel the
evil presence and the cold of evil—all eight of us did. The
evil was still there, especially in the guest bedroom.

After working our way through every room in the
house, we sat together in the living room and prayed
some more. We specifically prayed for Roxanne and for
the staff at the ministry home she was in. We finally had
a strong feeling that our home was clean and free and no
longer haunted. I thanked everyone for coming over and
spending their evening praying with us and ridding our
home of evil spirits.

An hour later it was time for bed. This time I felt I was
going to bed in a clean home. I locked the doors, turned
out all the lights, and got under the covers. I was about to
enjoy what I was positive would be a long night of nothing but deep sleep. I remember smiling happily.

Then I felt the evil presence again. This could not be
happening! It had to be my imagination. I refused to be-

lieve that the power of evil was greater than the power of God. We had commanded every evil thing to leave in Jesus' name. We had anointed our doors with oil, a symbol of the Holy Spirit's presence. I could see the translucent shape of the cross above the door in my bedroom. Based on everything I had been taught since childhood about God's omnipotence, there was no way our home should still be haunted.

But the malignant presence grew stronger until it was the most intense feeling of evil I had experienced so far.

I felt my heart skip a beat and then a full body shudder coming on. But it was like waiting for a reluctant sneeze. I sat up in bed, tense, holding my breath, looking around to see what might be there, but hoping like crazy I would see nothing.

Then something started hitting my feet, first gently and then really hard. I was sitting up but couldn't see over the edge of the bed. But I refused to move even an inch closer.

"Honey, are you awake?" I called out.

"Yes, why?" my wife answered back groggily. I had awakened her.

"Are you hitting my feet and legs?" I asked, already knowing the answer.

Now she sat up and responded, "Of course not."

"Honey, something is hitting my feet and legs," I said, my emotions too numb to allow me to speak with anything more than a deadpan tone.

She turned on the lights and we both leaned forward and looked over the foot of the bed. Nothing was there. She looked at me puzzled. Her expression made me wonder for the first time in a week if I was finally and officially losing my mind. But what I felt was real. It was not a pressing or a slight tap or even a light hit; this was a hard knock each time. Something had been hitting my legs. We left the bedroom light on all night. It seemed to help, but I still didn't sleep much.

The next night was a repeat performance. No sooner were the lights out and I was under the covers than I felt the dark, evil presence. It's hard to explain how that feels, but there is no mistaking it once you feel it, and no one has to explain it to you. I remember watching the ceiling fan going around, praying and asking God to save us. After a while I could see faint traces of light and vapor spinning around the ceiling fan. Were my eyes just blurring? I couldn't make out shapes or even colors. The only way I can explain what was happening is to say that I felt the evil presence through my eyes.

We had gathered with friends to pray in Jesus' name, but rather than getting better, things were getting worse.

As I continued to see shapes spin and dart above my bed, I closed my eyes tightly and began to pray: "In Jesus' name, you must leave this room."

There was little power or conviction in my voice, but when I looked up the shapes were gone. I thought about getting up and turning off the light. However, the evil presence was still strong. All I could do was struggle to breathe.

My wife and I looked at each other. I think we saw the discouragement in each other's eyes and felt even more despair. Just days before we had dropped Roxanne off at a home for troubled youth and thought we were getting our lives back. Now we were terrified, exhausted, and confused. The battle was supposed to be over. How could our home be haunted? Didn't we have a God-ordained authority to command these spirits to leave our house and leave us alone?

At this moment I was really beginning to wonder if we were ever going to be free from the demonic activity that had entered our lives through working with Roxanne.

It was 2:00 a.m. and we couldn't take it anymore. I looked at my wife and said, "We need to leave right now."

There was no argument from her. We got up, put on street clothes, packed a change of clothes and toiletries, and ran across the yard to our next-door neighbors' house. I rang the doorbell as I pounded on the door. When I explained to our good friends what was happening, they immediately opened their guest room for us and told us we could stay as long as we needed. I was so glad to be out of my house.

We slept like babies at our friends' home. I had forgotten how wonderful sleep felt and what a peaceful feeling was like. No doors slammed; nothing hit my feet. I didn't see traces of light and vapor flying through the air. The bathroom light stayed off all night long—except when I got up and turned it on to use the bathroom. I went to work refreshed.

We were incredibly relieved that the demons hadn't come with us. They were in our house but had not clung to us when we went next door. That was the good news.

The bad news was that no matter how kind and gracious our neighbors were, we all knew we couldn't live in their guest room indefinitely—and our house was still apparently filled with active and malignant demons despite our prayers.

To this day I do not fully understand this. I'm not a

theologian, and so I try to stay clear of making theological pronouncements. I can report only what I witnessed. As stated already, from my observation, Roxanne had made a clear and sincere profession of faith and renounced the evil inside her, most notably the demon Lacey. I also observed that demons were still in and around her life, despite my belief that an evil spirit cannot inhabit the body of a child of God. I wondered whether an individual suffering from a multiple-personality disorder could have a saved personality and a demon-possessed personality sharing the same body. I still don't have a satisfactory answer to these questions.

Likewise, I believed then, and still do, that demons must submit to orders given by a child of God in Jesus' name. Jesus said: "Assuredly, I say to you, if you have faith as a mustard seed, you will say to this mountain, 'Move from here to there,' and it will move; and nothing will be impossible for you" (Matt. 17:20).

I am confident I had at least some faith. But the demons did not obey.

Would this be a mystery that would not be solved until I stood before Jesus Christ in heaven?

CHAPTER 11

What Was Under the Bed?

We stayed with our friends for the next couple of nights. We walked back and forth to our house to pick up things we needed. We rarely went inside alone. And in broad daylight only, never after dark. We weren't sure what to do. Should we just leave the home and look for another place to live? We were stretched to the limit on payments and the lease wasn't up, so leaving the house empty and renting another place was not a feasible option.

We could return and pray over the house again. With more friends this time? After all, we had to pray with Roxanne numerous times before she accepted Jesus Christ. But she still seemed to have demons in her life, so I wasn't sure that was the best idea.

I had a short out-of-town trip coming up. My house was located close to our airport. Dave, a coworker who was going with me, asked if he could spend the night at my house so we could leave together. He would leave his car there, thus saving the parking fee. He didn't know we hadn't been staying in our home. He apparently didn't really understand what was going on there and in our lives despite hearing the stories.

I explained to Dave that the house was haunted and asked him if he still wanted to stay the night.

To my surprise he didn't seem to have a problem with it. Again, I think it was because he really didn't understand how bad it was. Or he may have been polite but skeptical of my stories and didn't believe the home was haunted and was out to prove it. I had heard rumors that people were beginning to worry about me and if I was in my right mind.

This was now week three of Roxanne being gone and our house being haunted. We couldn't live out of a suitcase forever, and since we had a good Christian friend who had volunteered to sleep in our home, we decided to move back in for the night. My wife would go back to our neighbors' house when I was away, and then later we would see if we could pray ourselves back into the house that had at one time felt like a gift from God.

I began to get a bad feeling as my workday came to a close. I would have preferred to stay at work rather than go home, knowing there was only so much sunlight left in the day and then the insanity of living in a haunted house might begin again. I was pleased Dave was coming to spend the night. Perhaps nothing would happen. If something did, it would be good to have the extra support. We all had a nice meal together and spent the evening catching up. Then we prayed for Roxanne. Dave had been part of the original core group—but he hadn't been close to the recurring problems we'd experienced since Roxanne left our home. So while he was somewhat aware of the forces that swirled around Roxanne, he wasn't up to date on our latest battles.

My wife and I were concerned about the sleeping arrangements, but he insisted that as a child of God he feared no evil and was happy to sleep in the room where Roxanne had stayed.

When it was time for bed, we again prayed together, and then went to our separate rooms for the night.

Was the evil presence gone? I didn't think so. In check? Maybe. But I could feel something beneath the apparent surface of tranquillity. Amazingly, nothing happened that night. Nothing. All night. At least not in our bedroom. Wow. Did we have our house back?

The next morning we were sitting at the breakfast table when Dave came out to join us. He looked flustered and said in a strained voice, "I had the craziest night of my life. I apologize for doubting you. You are right, your home is haunted."

Really? My wife and I looked at each other, confused. We hadn't heard a thing.

"What happened?" I asked.

Dave said that he was lying on the bed facedown, just about to fall asleep, when something jumped onto the bed.

"At first I thought it was a dog, even though I knew you didn't have a dog," he said. "Something was on my back, pushing my head into the pillow. It wasn't that heavy, so I tried to push myself up to knock it off me, but then I couldn't move at all.

"I started to panic," he continued. "I couldn't move at all by now, and it was getting difficult to breathe. Then whatever it was started pushing my face harder into the pillow. I think it was planning to suffocate me."

We were still speechless. My wife finally rasped out the question: "How did you get free?"

Dave was one of those guys with a ton of energy and a great sense of humor. But now he was quite still. He spoke without his usual animated style that included lots of volume and hand motions.

"With my mouth crushed down in the pillow, I couldn't speak out loud," he said, "but in my mind, I began to pray: *In Jesus' name, get off me and leave this room.* I was getting light-headed and desperate, so after a while all I could do was repeat the name Jesus over and over. Suddenly, whatever it was let up, and I felt it bounce off the bed in two big steps. I jumped up and turned on the light, but it was gone.

"Your house is haunted," Dave said again, no longer skeptical.

The three of us left the house at the same time, my wife for work with plans to spend the night at our friends; Dave and I for the airport.

I have to admit it was good to be gone for a few days to escape because, even without Roxanne in my home, we still had big troubles. I had no clue how to deal with a haunted house. My business trip ended too quickly. I went straight home from the airport with the familiar sense of dread. Quoting Scripture, I walked from room to room. Things didn't feel particularly strange, but the really weird feelings and bizarre activities usually didn't happen until after dark.

I was really hoping that for whatever reason the evil spirits had decided to move out while we were gone so we didn't have to face them again. The relative calm of the moment made me wonder if the house might really be safe. I should have known better. The worst night yet was almost upon us.

Bedtime neared. My wife was coping by keeping very busy, either doing something in the house or concentrating on reading a book. When we hit the bed she was out like a light. Her breathing was peaceful. I thought to myself that this might be a good sign, but no sooner did that thought enter my mind than I felt the evil presence again. Every hair on my body seemed to be standing on end, and I could feel a chill, even though I was deep under the covers.

I knew something was different, more intense tonight. Something had jumped on Dave the last night we had been back in our house, which was the boldest step yet by the demons. Were they going to make a similar or even more aggressive move toward me?

I could feel the evil getting thicker, drawing closer every minute. My eyes were open, but I didn't see anything. Yet the presence was real, physical, and palpable.

"Dear God, be our Protector," I began to pray. I knew we had reached a new level of spiritual and physical danger this time. Each passing minute the evil seemed stronger and more intense. While it wasn't the first time I had ever had a difficult time breathing, I think I have had a small glimpse into how someone with a severe respiratory illness feels when they are having an acute episode. Suddenly, I felt like I had weights on my chest. I was terrified but unable to move. But there is no inhaler to put on your bedside to handle spiritual oppression.

Then my wife sat bolt upright and looked into the mirror on our dresser to the left of the bed. If you looked in the mirror, you could see the reflection of the door and hallway, which was to the right of the bed. She looked at me with blank eyes and lay back down.

"What did you see?" I gasped between breaths.

"Nothing," she said. "I'm just dreaming."

I knew she wasn't dreaming, and she did, too, but she was too afraid to admit it. I struggled to sit up but couldn't. My breathing was now really distressed.

"What did you see?" I whispered hoarsely.

She sat back up and looked in the mirror again. When she turned toward me, she was careful not to let her eyes look above me. She didn't want to look directly at what she had seen reflected in the mirror.

We were both in bad shape, each on the verge of a panic attack.

She still hadn't answered, so I said with as much strength and urgency as I could muster, "You're not dreaming! Tell me what you see in the hallway."

She whispered, "There is a black figure walking down the hall toward our bedroom."

Terror swept over me. I couldn't move and wasn't sure I could even speak. I remembered Dave saying he prayed in his mind because he was suffocating.

My wife whispered again, "It has stopped and is standing outside our door."

Later she was able to recount that she was sure the figure wasn't a person but something spiritual, a demon.

"Please do something," she said to me.

Whether it is finances, physical threats, or spiritual warfare, there is no worse feeling for a man than to know he does not have the strength to protect his family. At that moment, I did not have the strength.

My breathing was still distressed and my body would not obey commands my mind gave it. I prayed, "In Jesus' name, you must leave. You cannot enter here." As I grew more light-headed I said more loudly, "Jesus, save us and protect us." And then I followed Dave's lead and just repeated the name of my Lord, "Jesus," over and over.

My manly pride would prefer to tell you how I stood tall and pointed at the spirit and with a strong voice commanded it to leave. But I was flat on my back and couldn't even see the door. My wife was the one sitting up and telling me what was happening.

"He's backing up," she said. "Keep praying."

I believe my faith was strong at this moment, but all I felt was fear.

As I prayed under the covers I asked my wife what was happening. She said that the figure was walking backward, away from our bedroom, and added, "Don't stop praying now!"

So I continued to pray and somehow found my voice again. I repeated "Jesus protect us," and "You must leave in Jesus' name," until she let out a yelp and said, "It's gone!"

Those were the best words I had ever heard. You could feel the evil presence lifting as the demon disappeared into the night. My breathing returned to normal and I was able to sit up.

It was the middle of the night, but my wife and I got out of bed to go sit in the living room. Who could sleep after experiencing something like that? It seemed as soon as I thought things could not get any crazier, they did just that. I think my credulity was already stretched to the breaking point at work, even with some who had prayed over Roxanne with us. Who was I going to be able to tell that my wife saw a black figure at the door of our bedroom and then retreating down our hallway? After almost four weeks of this insanity, we were totally exhausted on every level of our being! We sat in the living room with all the lights in the house burning brightly. My wife was sobbing and I just stared forward blankly, more frustrated than I had ever been in my life.

After a while she fell asleep on the sofa. I continued to sit there, reflecting on the strange happenings of the last month. The battles we had fought, the demons we had heard and my wife had seen with her own eyes. I was overwhelmed by the power of evil. But even though I was deeply discouraged, I was aware that I still hadn't let go of my faith in God. I continued to believe in His power. Living in a haunted house, I didn't feel that we were winning any battles. But the fact that Roxanne had prayed to accept Christ and renounced evil in her life said otherwise. I had a sudden strong impression of God's presence, and at that precise moment, all I could do was worship Him. I was captivated by His love and power.

As my wife slept on the sofa and I reflected, prayed, and feared what might be next, something happened that was even more bizarre than anything that had occurred earlier that evening.

I looked down the hallway. There stood the black figure. But that's not what was most bizarre. What was most bizarre—at least to me looking back at that moment in my life—was that I wasn't afraid of it.

Someone might explain my reaction as perhaps a result of the new and eerie experiences I had gone through and therefore I could no longer be shocked. Others might conclude I was burned out by the lack of sleep. But to this day I know that what was different was me. I had experienced God. I had been to church in my living room. I had praised and worshipped the Creator God of the universe and glorified Him for His love, His compassion, His goodness, His faithfulness, and His mercies.

All these years later I am still amazed at what I did next. I stood up and walked straight toward the black figure. I figured the worst that could happen was it would kill me, and at this point, that was okay because I couldn't take living in a state of constant fear and dread anymore—but I also had felt a glimpse of heaven, of being in the presence of the living God. I really did feel peace at the thought of dying. I think for the first time I understood Job's prayer after God allowed Satan to take everything from him, including house, health, riches, and family: "Though He slay me, yet will I trust Him. Even so, I will defend my own ways before Him" (Job 13:15).

I walked up to this shrouded, faceless figure. I looked straight at it and asked, "Why do you feel you can come into my home? What makes you think you have the right?"

The demon did not flinch but answered in a very clear voice, "I'm an invited guest in this home."

A what? I almost said aloud. I knew neither my wife nor I had invited a demon inside our home, and Roxanne was not here. Five minutes earlier his response would have thrown me for a loop, but I still tingled with God's presence. I felt His love and protection over my life and my body. I wasn't going to be cowed or back down.

I looked at him and boldly commanded, "In Jesus' name, tell me how you think you are an invited guest in this house."

He answered just as loudly and clearly as the first time, "Haven't you looked under Roxanne's bed?"

I gasped. Not in fear, but with the feeling you get when you've forgotten an important appointment or to follow through on something you promised you would take care of.

I remembered having the strong impression that I

should look under Roxanne's bed. I rationalized not doing anything at the time by dismissing the voice as a manifestation of my fear. Now I wasn't so sure that ignoring it hadn't been an act of prideful disobedience on my part, caring more about my feelings than God's promptings. I truly had depended on God throughout this ordeal, and I'm now positive this omission was a manifestation of my pride. It was taking a demon to confirm that the voice heard was clearly the Holy Spirit telling me to check under Roxanne's bed.

I calmly replied to the demon, "You are no longer welcome here; you will leave this house in Jesus' name. Now."

There was no violent outburst. No taunting. No response at all. The black figure walked to the front door and, as God is my witness, walked right through it and left.

I now knew exactly what I had to do in order to get my house back and be rid of demonic activity. The Lord was obviously telling me that there was something evil under Roxanne's bed. I walked into the guest room where she had stayed and reached under the bed without even bending over to look. My hands immediately found and pulled out a bunch of Roxanne's witchcraft paraphernalia. I found a robe she had worn as a witch in the coven, some books, jewelry, and a few other things that I couldn't identify, but seemed to be part of her dark past.

It was 3:00 a.m., but this couldn't wait for morning. I had to get everything that had anything to do with Roxanne out of my home immediately.

What do you do with objects that are consecrated to Satan? Put them in a big black trash bag and take them to the dump? That didn't feel quite "permanent" enough. I took everything to the back porch and grabbed some items from the garage.

First I smashed the jewelry with a hammer. If the neighbors had looked out their window and seen me hammering away in the moonlight, they would have thought I'd gone certifiably crazy. I put the fragments in a trash bag.

Next I got Roxanne's robe and placed it on the grill. I poured lighter fluid on it and lit it with a match. The flame was as bright as you would expect, but the robe wouldn't burn. I watched as the fire continued to burn, but still nothing was happening to the robe.

I might have known next to nothing of satanism and witchcraft, but I believed that divine words had divine power. So I stretched out my arms over the fire and prayed, in a loud voice: "In Jesus' name, you will burn!" At that very second the flames shot up and engulfed the robe. It seemed to disappear in a flash. It was like a movie producer had created special effects to make this moment incredibly dramatic, though I was witnessing a real event in real life.

As I looked into the grill at the dying embers, I discovered the robe hadn't quite disappeared. But there was nothing to suggest that a robe had been burned in the flames. What was left was a black rock. I threw it in the bag along with the remains of everything that had been in Roxanne's room.

Without thinking, I ran to Roxanne's car, opened the trunk, and threw in the bag. Why the car's trunk and not the trash can? I can only believe that I was being divinely directed, for as I stood in my driveway and I prayed that the Lord would show me anything else that needed to be destroyed and disposed of, right there was my answer—Roxanne's car.

Some will question if I had the right to destroy Roxanne's stuff. I didn't legally, I am sure, but I would do the same thing today, immediately and without guilt. Her car was a different matter. I wasn't going to torch it in my driveway. Not only would my neighbors have proof I had gone crazy, but the police might have had something to say about it as well.

I decided I at least had to get her old car off my driveway. I didn't want anything that might contain evil on my property, even if it was outside the four walls of my house.

Her car was old and beat up, and as I looked at it, I realized it was also a bit creepy. Don't ask me to explain how a car can look creepy; I can't. But it was.

I slowly opened the driver's door, praying for God's continued protection. The moment I slid into the driver's seat, I felt the presence of evil. I kept the door open with one leg outside the car just in case I had to make a quick escape. I'm sure my imagination was running on overdrive because of the popular Stephen King novel and movie that feature a demon-possessed car. I was ready to bolt if that engine suddenly roared to life and the headlights cut a path into the night darkness!

As I sat down to start the car, I froze. Something—not a voice this time, but still a very strong impression—told me not to look in the rearview mirror. I knew I was not alone. Something, some presence, was in the backseat.

Have your eyes ever been drawn to something you shouldn't look at? Many of us have felt the irresistible urge to stare at an accident scene, even though our minds and brains tell us we are slowing down traffic, it's none of our business, and it would be safer to keep our eyes on the road.

I almost always look. Except this time I resisted and refused to look in the mirror. Did it matter? Would something bad have happened to me, or some evil presence gained access to my heart if I had looked? I'll never know. I just know that at that moment, it seemed to be the most important thing in the world for me not to look if I was to finally get rid of the evil that had been "invited" into my life and home.

I backed out of the drive by memory and drove the car to the end of the road, which was a dead end, and shifted into Park. I locked the car doors and walked away from the vehicle without ever having looked in the backseat. The sense of a malignant presence near me didn't let up as I walked away, so I suddenly broke into a mad dash to my house. I entered through the front door, slammed it shut, and quickly turned the dead bolt.

Obviously worn out from the night's activities, my wife was still sleeping on the living room couch. I can't believe that none of my activities, especially slamming the door shut, woke her.

Finally, the car was gone, all of Roxanne's stuff was off our property, and the house was hopefully demon-free. I wasn't certain what would happen when we went back to bed. We had hoped and believed that the worst was behind us numerous times in the last month, only to discover that the worst was yet to be.

I woke my wife, not wanting her to be in the living room by herself if the house was still not free of evil. I told her briefly of what I had done with Roxanne's belongings as we walked down the hall. She was so tired she just nodded as we went to bed for the second time that night.

I turned out the lights and waited. Would I feel a bump against my foot? Would I see something walking through the house? Would doors start slamming again? Would the bathroom light turn on and off? Would I hear voices and conversations? Would I hear knocks and bumps and creaks throughout the house?

What I heard was nothing. Absolutely nothing. Nothing made sounds and nothing happened in the final hours before daylight. All I could do was praise God! Lying on my back, I said, "Thank You, Jesus," again and again. The house was clean. The demons were gone.

I learned that night that any open door in your life, whatever form it takes, can provide access to demonic activity. Yes, as a child of God, I had the authority to command demons to leave my home. But if Satan is given the opportunity to return, he will. As I've already said, I'm not a theologian, and I'm also not a psychiatrist. In the years since this experience I've read books on demonic possession and exorcism and learned a little about the psychological illness involving multiple personalities (dissociative identity disorder or multiple personality disorder). I have now come to believe that Roxanne's heart was a revolving door of demons' being cast out and re-entering through her multiple personalities. I'll leave it to the theologians to explain her spiritual state before God while all this was happening to her, but I know His grace is sufficient, even for such a complex person as Roxanne. The line is blurred for me, and I wonder whether there was ever a moment of true freedom from satanic activity in her life.

I likewise believe similar dynamics were at work in my home. Each morning and evening we would pray earnestly—and maybe even effectively—for our home to be cleansed and for all evil to leave in Jesus' name. I don't know for sure, but maybe the demons would actually leave for a moment. However, the door guarding our house and lives was wide open because of all the satanic paraphernalia under Roxanne's bed.

Some theologians would question whether evil and evil spirits can inhabit inanimate objects. There's no question in my mind that Satan can possess more than live human beings. Didn't Jesus send a legion of demons from a man into a herd of pigs?

> *A large herd of pigs was feeding on the nearby hillside. The demons begged Jesus, "Send us among the pigs; allow us to go into them." He gave them permission, and the impure spirits came out and went into the pigs. The herd, about two thousand in number, rushed down the steep bank into the lake and were drowned.* (Mark 5:11–13 NIV)

I believe the materials under Roxanne's bed, and the presence of her car in our driveway, gave the demons access to our home and caused fear, anxiety, distress, and even physical pain.

There is no question that Satan is at work in the world today, and I believe this occurs primarily through the influence and temptations of "fallen people." That alone should be enough for us to make a decision to get rid of some music, magazines, and books and block certain channels available on our TV sets. That doesn't mean you and I are going to agree completely on what is clearly evil and perverted and what is harmless or at least thought-provoking and informational.

But beyond these general thoughts about what we allow into our homes, there is a whole other category: items that have clearly been ordained for satanic use. Don't stop to check your conscience. Get rid of any item sanctified for evil immediately.

The Holy Spirit tried to tell me something evil was under Roxanne's bed, and at first I didn't listen. That would never be the case for me again—and I pray the same is true for you.

My house was finally clean. I felt at peace and looked forward to coming home for the first time in a month.

Would our lives get back to normal now?

CHAPTER 12

The Search for Roxanne

Roxanne was in the program for troubled young adults, and the house was no longer haunted. Life seemed to be returning to normal. That was my hope and prayer.

Most important, I had learned not only to depend on God in spiritual warfare, but how vital it is to praise and worship God in the midst of any battle. You might remember the story of Jesus sending out the seventy-two to minister in His name. But do you know that upon their return Jesus told them that there's something even more important than having authority over demons?

> The seventy returned with joy, saying, "Lord, even the demons are subject to us in Your name." And He said to them, "I saw Satan fall like lightning from heaven. Behold, I give you the authority to trample on serpents and scorpions, and over all the power of the enemy, and nothing shall by any means hurt you. Nevertheless do not rejoice in this, that the spirits are subject to you, but rather rejoice because your names are written in heaven." (Luke 10:17–20)

The authority that comes from trusting God is a wonderful gift. But the joy that Jesus most wants us to experience is having our names written in heaven. That is the joy of worshipping the One with whom we will spend eternity.

I continued to praise God in a new and deeper way. This made me even more determined to win the battle for Roxanne. With time now to finally reflect a bit, I began to realize that things didn't really add up as far as who Roxanne represented herself to be.

Who was this girl? I should really ask, Who was this woman? I still sometimes automatically thought of her as Lacey, a young frightened teen. I wondered what her exact age was.

I had many questions circling in my mind. Just how deep in the occult did she go? Was she a high priestess in a satanic coven or just a big talker, or both?

I decided to begin actively searching for information and answers. Roxanne had a box of stuff in her car. I thought that would be a great place to begin my search for any clues about who this woman really was. I remembered the overwhelming sense that there was a presence in the backseat, so I made sure that it was broad daylight before walking down the street to her car. The car door creaked and groaned as I tried to open it. I flinched back. But the sun was shining brightly, so I pressed on. I asked God to protect me in mind, body, and spirit.

The inside of the car was a mess. It was hard to know where to begin, so I just grabbed whatever was closest to me. I sorted through a lot of junk that didn't tell me much—fast-food wrappers and trash appeared to be the only things inside. I was about ready to give up. Then I thought to look in the glove compartment.

I removed a little black notebook. What I saw when I opened it surprised me. There was a list of people's names, addresses, and phone numbers, with dates beside each one that went back ten years.

Interesting, I thought. *What could this be?* Maybe it was a list of witches and warlocks or members of her coven. How dangerous could this information be for me to have? Roxanne said members of the coven would come looking for her and that no one was allowed to leave at her level. She said they always caught up with and killed any deserters so their secrets couldn't be revealed to the outside world. I took the notebook inside the house—praying God's protection over my wife and I and knowing it needed to be taken back outside immediately after we looked at it. I showed the notebook to my wife.

I'm not the kind of guy who would normally go through people's personal belongings. I've never even peeked inside someone else's journal. But with all we had gone through and with all that Roxanne had to overcome, I didn't feel wrong or uncomfortable searching for clues to understand and better help Roxanne.

My wife and I agreed there could be important information we needed inside this book. We decided I should do the most obvious thing we could think of, which was to start calling numbers and ask whoever answered if they knew Roxanne.

There were ten years' worth of names and numbers recorded chronologically, not alphabetically. So where should we begin? Earliest or latest date? And what if I talked to a leader of a satanic cult and accidentally gave away information that would lead to Roxanne or my wife?

I prayed, "Lord, give me the right number to call."

I called a random name and number. I could hear the phone ringing and my heart skipped a beat with each ring. I was about to hang up on the seventh or eighth ring when a man answered the phone with a simple "Hello."

I asked if the number belonged to the man listed in the book. He answered affirmatively and asked what he could do for me.

I paused at this point. *What could he do for me?* Why was I calling him? He thought maybe we had lost the connection and asked if I was still there.

"Hi, my name is Bill," I blurted out. "We have had a young lady living with us named Roxanne. I found your number in a notebook of hers and wanted to see if you know her."

Now it was his turn to pause. I knew he was still on the line but asked if he was there anyway just to break the silence.

The phone was silent. This could not be a good sign.

"Hello?" I asked again.

The man replied in a quiet voice, "Do you have Roxanne now?"

I didn't want to blurt out yes in case he meant her or me harm. I had no idea who this man was yet.

"We don't have her right now, but she is in a safe place," I responded. "We are trying to help her."

I don't know who was being more cautious with their words, this man or me.

"Are you in ministry?" he asked.

His question hit me like an electrical shock. Was I dealing with another demon-possessed person who knew what was going on in remote places? But I didn't sense an evil presence about him.

"Yes," I answered, my voice quivering a little.

"I am the pastor of a church in Indiana," he said.

"What?" I wanted to shout at him. How in the world could this man be a pastor? Roxanne said she'd never had contact with Christians before. The pastor could tell I was surprised by his response.

"About five years ago Roxanne called us for help," he said. "We brought her into our home, which was the biggest mistake I ever made. I hope you haven't done the same. You never want to let a demon-possessed person into your house."

My wife had been leaning in during the conversation and was able to hear his words. We looked at each other in amazement.

"I'm afraid your advice is a little too late," I said to him with a half laugh. "She did live with us and brought everything inside her into our home."

"I'm so sorry," he said.

"It's okay now," I responded. "Roxanne is no longer here. She really is in a safe place with good folks who know how to work with troubled people."

"Do they really?" he asked rhetorically. "Let me ask you, How much do you know about witchcraft and the occult and demon possession?"

"Not much," I admitted to him. I told him almost everything I had learned over the last five weeks. His response did not help the uneasy feelings I already had.

"Son, I have been in the ministry of spiritual deliverance for twenty-five years. I have never encountered anyone like Roxanne and the level of demons that control her life. Be careful."

What followed was a simple primer on the ministry of exorcism. He shared that there are different levels of demons, some more powerful than others. Roxanne was possessed with the most powerful demons he had ever encountered. He said that every demon is subject to the power of Jesus Christ, but the stronger demons are more canny and better able to avoid direct confrontation with Jesus through manipulation and intimidation of anyone who would dare stand up to them.

I had already come to understand this in part, but these were still not the words I wanted to hear. What might happen to the workers who were ministering to her even as we spoke? I quickly told Pastor Cliff—we had made more formal introductions by this point—everything that had happened to us since the day Satan called my radio hotline in the voice of a helpless little girl named Lacey. I let him know where Roxanne was staying now and asked if he would lead in prayer for the safety of the teens, young adults, and workers who were around Roxanne night and day.

He prayed and then told us some stories of his time with Roxanne.

"My wife and I took Roxanne into our home for five months. Esther and I would pray over her late every night. We were experienced in spiritual warfare and would bind the demons that were in her through the name and blood of Jesus. But one night we were praying and the demons were so furious with us that the house began to shake. The battle was that powerful. The evil spirits were tormented by our prayers to the point that they shook our home in rage. I've never been in an earthquake, but I think I know what one feels like now.

"Later that year, Roxanne left and went back home to Louisiana," Pastor Cliff told us. "I was in a regular meeting with my church board and Roxanne's name came up. One of the elders suggested that we pray for her, so we did. I don't know exactly how many miles away she was in Louisiana, but as we prayed the same thing happened in the church that happened in my house. The building began to shake as if we were in an earthquake. Indiana isn't known for earthquakes, but this was my second one since meeting Roxanne.

"Everyone in the meeting was upset, but then we heard a voice boom out of thin air. It screamed at us, 'Why do you torment me so?!'

"A lot of us had been knocked out of our chairs already. But when we heard that, let me tell you, we all hit the floor, faces down, calling out to God to protect us."

If I had talked to Pastor Cliff on the phone a little more than a month before that, I would have thought he was crazy. I would have been polite by agreeing with him, but I'm not sure I would have believed him. I might have considered that something like this was possible. But not probable enough for me to even take an elderly pastor who claimed to have spent twenty-five years of his ministry battling demons at his word.

Pastor Cliff asked if I had talked to Abaddon yet.

"I don't know, but I don't think so," I answered.

"Well, maybe you did and maybe you didn't, but you'd probably know," he said. "He's powerful and crafty. Once someone gets close to him with the name of Jesus, he usually moves Roxanne somewhere else."

Moves Roxanne? Was this a pattern? Had this happened to others besides Pastor Cliff and me?

"How will I know I have met Abaddon?" I asked.

"You'll know," he said in a soft voice. "Just like there's other things you've known but couldn't explain."

My heart sank. Pastor Cliff was speaking as though our battle was not over. He was warning me about what was to come. I thought the battle was behind us, and if we saw Roxanne again it would be with her as a new person in Christ. I thought again of Paul's beautiful words about becoming a Christian: "If anyone is in Christ, he is a new creation; old things have passed away; behold, all things have become new" (2 Cor. 5:17).

I was more than ready to behold all things new—not face a renewed spiritual warfare even greater than what I had already experienced!

After agreeing to stay in touch and pray for each other, we hung up. I continued to look through the notebook and call numbers. There was no better way to get a more complete picture of Roxanne than to talk to people she had spent time with over the previous decade.

During the next week I spent hours on the phone talking with people who had met Roxanne and tried to help her. There were pastors, nice couples who were always ready to open their home to a person in need, and directors and staff members from a variety of ministries, even Christian radio.

Everyone I talked to whose name was in this notebook was a Christian motivated by Christian love. But by the third call I noted an emerging pattern—a chilling and unmistakable theme in all these conversations. Everywhere Roxanne had been, a battlefield littered with broken relationships was left behind. I was told about a church split, at least several divorces among those who were closest to Roxanne, and other devastating consequences. Every place Roxanne had visited experienced chaos.

Could I be hearing this? Roxanne had told me herself that one of her coven's top priorities was the breakup of Christian marriages. Very few events spill over and damage the faith of others more than a divorce. And I've heard more than a few leaders say that a church split almost always damages the faith and attendance of an entire congregation—usually the youth and young adults.

It should be no surprise that broken relationships damage our Christian witness. It was Jesus that taught His disciples the opposite—that the greatest witness to the faith is unity: "By this all will know that you are My disciples, if you have love for one another" (John 13:35).

Was Roxanne sent from a satanic coven to destroy churches, ministries, and Christian couples? Any claim I make is based on anecdotal evidence. But even as prevalent as divorce among Christians and church conflict are, I had never gone through conversation after conversation with this as a common theme, before or since. And the constant presence in all these stories was Roxanne.

You can imagine the concern I felt for what I had gotten my wife and myself into—though it never crossed my mind at the time that my marriage would ever be at risk.

I never asked Pastor Cliff if he was advising me not to work with Roxanne anymore. There's a good chance I wouldn't have listened had he tried. I still wasn't ready to give up on Roxanne.

I really did believe that inside her was a beautiful person ready to emerge. Even if she had been a destructive force in previous church experiences, what if this was finally the moment she was ready to experience the full saving grace of God? How much more of a force for good and reconciliation could she be then?

The search for the real Roxanne seemed to have begun. I had even found a few answers. But it seemed the more I learned about her, the less I knew her.

CHAPTER 13

Something Bad Is Happening

Was ministering to Roxanne the most difficult thing I had ever undertaken? Of course. But Jesus described Himself as a shepherd, and He put all His efforts into saving just one lost sheep (Luke 15:1-7). In Psalm 23 we read that He leads us into green pastures and beside gentle streams (v. 2)—but Jesus doesn't stay in the peaceful places when one of His sheep has wandered into the steep, rocky hillsides of life. And doesn't John 3:16 say: "For God so loved the world that He gave His only begotten Son, that whoever believes in Him should not perish but have everlasting life"?

"Whoever" included Roxanne, right? As discouraging and disheartening as the reports of her past were, I knew that we needed to keep fighting for this woman. No matter what level of power these demons possessed, including Abaddon, God's power was greater—and as His child, that power was available to me. I believed that with all my heart. I still do.

In going through the notebook I discovered that Roxanne had been enrolled in seven other programs for disturbed youth over the previous ten years. The helpless girl who was afraid of being sacrificed by members of her coven on Halloween knew what she was doing.

At the end of a week of phone calls, I knew I had better call the group home where Roxanne was living to see how they were doing—and at least attempt to impress on them the seriousness of this new information I had collected. They weren't her first stop.

I called the director, and he told me Roxanne was doing well and had not caused any problems. This was almost shocking after what I had just learned. Maybe this was Roxanne's moment to finally break free. I told him that this wasn't the first group home she had lived in and that there was a pattern of destruction in the wake of her stays. He just said he'd take it under advisement and then asked when we would be able to visit Roxanne since we were her only "family." I told him to let me discuss it with my wife and I would get back to him.

A couple of nights later, I was walking through the living room when all of a sudden I had a strong feeling that God was saying to me, *Get on your knees. Start praying for Roxanne and the staff and those other participants now. Something bad is happening.*

I hadn't heard the audible voice of the Creator of the universe. But what I felt was very real and made a physical impression on me. It was not just the gentle nudging to move in the right direction. This "voice" hit me with a sense of urgency. It was a command. I had already made a commitment to myself and to God that if I heard His voice again, I was going to do whatever He asked me to do. I had learned a hard life lesson from ignoring the voice of the Holy Spirit telling me to look under Roxanne's bed.

I dropped to my knees right there, right then. I began to pray fervently for the safety of the leaders at the program, those being treated in the program, and Roxanne.

Like anyone who has ever thought deeply about the spiritual act of prayer, I don't know why God seems to need us to pray. I know God needs nothing from us at all. He is holy, perfect, complete, all-powerful, and able to do whatever He wants. But in His design He created us to pray, not only for the benefit it brings to our own lives, but also to see His will done in and around us.

I was no prayer warrior. Unlike Pastor Cliff, I was also no expert on demon oppression and possession. But that night, I prayed hard and began to bind the demons. I am not known for saying long prayers, but at that moment I prayed for what felt like a very long time.

While praying I heard the phone ring. My wife answered. It was the director of the group home. She looked into the living room and saw me on my knees praying. "You need to take this phone call; something's going on at the group home with Roxanne," she said urgently.

I really did hear from God. That was a great feeling in such a confusing time. I was glad that I had listened and got down on my knees when I did. I picked up the phone and said hello to Roxanne's house monitor. She was one of the "tough" ladies I had met on our visit. By the tone of her voice, I knew immediately something was very wrong.

"Roxanne has demons," she blurted out. "This girl is possessed."

"What's happened?" I asked, not sure I really wanted to know.

"Roxanne isn't Roxanne," she said. "She has everyone terrified. Just a few minutes ago she broke up our evening worship service. The last I saw she was running around the room swinging a chair over her head and cursing at each of us with a man's voice. Her eyes were rolled up into the back of her head. But it wasn't just a man's voice coming out of her."

I explained to Roxanne's house monitor that I had been praying for her and Roxanne and everyone else just before she called.

"That's great," she answered. "But we need you to get out here right now. We need help."

I hung up and my wife and I quickly got ready to head to the center. While driving there I was thinking to myself that we all are in a battle with the spirit world. Most will never see it up close like this. But that doesn't mean demons are not real and fighting against us. We do live in a battlefield, even if we can't see all the fighting that takes place with our own eyes. Perhaps most Christians are a bit careless—or maybe a lot careless—when it comes to the battle for our souls and the souls of those around us—including our families. Paul told the Corinthian church:

Though we live in the world, we do not wage war as the world does. The weapons we fight with are not the weapons of the world. On the contrary, they have divine power to demolish strongholds. We demolish arguments and every pretension that sets itself up against the knowledge of God, and we take captive every thought to make it obedient to Christ. (2 Corinthians 10:3–5 NIV)

The apostle Paul also tells us:

Be strong in the Lord and in his mighty power.
Put on the full armor of God so that you can

take your stand against the devil's schemes. For our struggle is not against flesh and blood, but against the rulers, against the authorities, against the powers of this dark world and against the spiritual forces of evil in the heavenly realms. Therefore put on the full armor of God, so that when the day of evil comes, you may be able to stand your ground, and after you have done everything, to stand. Stand firm then, with the belt of truth buckled around your waist, with the breastplate of righteousness in place, and with your feet fitted with the readiness that comes from the gospel of peace. In addition to all this, take up the shield of faith, with which you can extinguish all the flaming arrows of the evil one. Take the helmet of salvation and the sword of the Spirit, which is the word of God. And pray in the Spirit on all occasions with all kinds of prayers and requests. With this in mind, be alert and always keep on praying for all the saints.
(Ephesians 6:10–18 NIV)

It was time to continue fighting, and as we drove I felt armed for the battle with the power of Scripture permeating my thoughts. The drive still seemed to go by way too quickly.

As we entered the main building we were met by two of the leaders, ashen-faced and wide-eyed. There was no time for small talk. I asked what Roxanne was doing now. I was told everyone had been sent back to their rooms, and it was just her and three of the leaders in the meeting room.

"Strange things are going on," the director began. "Tonight things came to a head in our worship service. But strange things really started a couple of days ago. In fact, it was the night you called."

I told him how God had impressed on me to pray for him and all the workers and participants at the center. I asked what strange things they were experiencing.

"Nothing has happened in the men's home, but the ladies' side is another matter. First there were reports of someone peeking in the windows. We thought it might be one of the boys sneaking out, but the next night it happened again. We knew all the guys were in their house. But then one of the ladies saw a face—and she swore it was not the face of a human.

"Roxanne had been so easy and delightful to work with, we really didn't think it had anything to do with her. But then we started hearing voices that we couldn't account for. And then a couple of the girls swore that things were jumping on them in the middle of the night. That's when we remembered all your warnings. I guess we should have listened."

I refrained from telling them what they were probably experiencing. "Everyone is terrified. We aren't sure what to do anymore. Probably time for you to come on in and see her. We need help."

We walked into the meeting room together. Roxanne looked up when I entered and hissed at me. She sounded like a ferocious cat that was ready to fight. Different voices tumbled out of her and cursed me. Just like before. I honestly wasn't afraid. But my first thought was rather self-serving. I hoped they wouldn't kick her out of the program. I didn't know what my wife and I would do with her.

Then she laid her head back and appeared to go to sleep or pass out. She was lying flat out on the floor, surrounded by those who had been praying for her. At this point we had no idea what was happening to Roxanne or what was going to happen next. This gave me the opportunity to walk through both houses with the staff. I imitated what I had seen others do in my home. I sent someone to the kitchen to find a bottle of oil. I told them any oil would work. The oil was symbolic of the blood of Christ and the Holy Spirit. Soon someone returned with simple cooking oil. With a little puddle of oil in the palm of one hand, I dipped my finger in and drew the sign of the cross over every door and window we passed. I asked them to pray with me and after me. We blessed every square foot of the houses, inside and out, in Jesus' name. When we came to an area where the students were, they looked at us with wide eyes. A lot of these participants had lived a much tougher life than I ever dreamed of in the shelter of my Christian home. But even guys who had a past with gangs were scared speechless.

We walked the property line, asking the Lord to send warrior angels to fight off anything evil that would come to this place of compassion and mercy. Now it was time to approach Roxanne.

When we returned to the meeting room, Roxanne's eyes were closed, but I had the feeling she wasn't asleep. I thought I saw a slight smirk in her expression. When she opened her eyes and screamed a blasphemy, all of us knew she was awake—including everyone who lived in the other house.

The staff at the center were experiencing what I had lived through for a month. One demon after another would scream they were going to kill Roxanne and us, too. I would rebuke each demon in Jesus' name, but one or more other demons would soon take up the litany of abuse and profanity.

One demon let a secret slip that I am not sure we were supposed to know. He said, "Eventually the witches will find her here." That let us know the humans searching for Roxanne could not find her. Apparently our prayers for protection were making a difference.

The first day Satan called, it was the demons telling us we couldn't have Lacey. Tonight it was me and my Christian brothers and sisters telling the demons they could not have Roxanne.

"In Jesus' name, you will not harm her. You must leave her. You are not welcome here. Leave in Jesus' name now."

Were a hundred demons familiar with Roxanne? A thousand? The revolving door of demons leaving and coming continued late into the night. Before tonight, this team of spiritual warriors sharing in the battle had thought I was crazy when I told them Roxanne was demon-possessed. Tonight the strength of their faith and commitment was evident as they boldly spoke against demons in Jesus' name—all doubts and reservations were removed. I felt tremendous power and support with this group. I do believe that special grace is given to those on the front lines of a difficult ministry, those who spend every day working with troubled individuals.

In between encounters with the demons, I shared everything I had learned in the short month of working with Roxanne, including the need to look through her belongings there.

As Roxanne calmed down and it appeared the evening of battle might be coming to a close, a low, powerful, commanding voice spoke from her. I was past shock by this point, but I knew something significant was happening when the hairs on my arms and on the back of my neck stood up. Roxanne stared at me. Though her eyes were no longer rolled back, I knew it was not Roxanne looking at me, but a demon. Holding eye contact with me, he said: "You believe that one day every tongue will confess that Jesus is Lord and that one day every knee will bow. Perhaps you are right. But I assure you, today is not that day."

His tone was almost aristocratic. He chuckled.

Roxanne slumped over as if she had passed out. The staff looked at me wide-eyed. I looked back at each one of them with wonder. Pastor Cliff said that I would know when I had encountered Abaddon. I was almost ready to assume I had just encountered him. But I had enough doubt that I took Pastor Cliff literally. He said there would be no doubt I had met him. So I still hadn't met Abaddon.

Roxanne looked up with a jolt and another demon's voice—not scary but almost pitiful—poured from her: "Don't send me away. Don't send me away, I beg of you. If I return to hell without this soul, my torment begins today."

Like the legion of demons that asked Jesus to send them into a herd of pigs, this demon begged us to send him into an animal or to ask Jesus to give him permission to wander.

We just prayed that he leave in the name and power of Jesus. I still didn't know that much about dealing with demons, so it was up to the Lord to tell him where he needed to go.

We spent the final hour praying over Roxanne and rebuking demons. There was peace with the first rays of morning light. She lifted herself up from where she had been lying on the floor. The focus in her eyes was back. It was Roxanne, not an evil spirit speaking through her. She asked the same question she had raised repeatedly since the night I had first met her in the office area of the church-based radio station I worked at: "What just happened?"

My new friends looked at me. I could only return their puzzled looks.

Was this a cunning way to make herself look innocent when she was actually the one who had orchestrated yet another terror-filled night? Maybe so. But she looked sincere and very innocent to me.

We told her a little of what had happened. She shook her head and tears rolled down her cheeks. The women hugged and comforted her and took her back to the room she stayed in to put her to bed.

We were all exhausted. It was time for my wife and I to head home so that I could have enough time to take a shower, get dressed, and head for work.

Amazing to me, the leadership team here was willing to continue working with Roxanne. What an answer to prayer that was. I believe they thought that the bigger the problem, the more they were needed.

As I drove home my thoughts returned to what Pastor Cliff had said about Abaddon. I was more and more certain he hadn't shown up.

I prayed I would never have to meet him face-to-face.

CHAPTER 14

Death Threats, Mad Cows, and the Disappearing Witch

I spoke with the director at the center every couple of days. We had become friends, but I still flinched when I heard his voice after picking up the phone. As much as I believed in the power of God to redeem Roxanne, I still expected he was calling with news of the worst.

There'd been no more incidents for a couple of weeks, and Roxanne was fully immersed in the program and doing well. She was learning more about the Bible and even sharing a little of her testimony when the group visited churches. These folks leading the program were braver than me. When I took Roxanne to church, she had growled and cursed at the people around her.

Was it possible she was free from the evil spirits that plagued her life? I wasn't even going to speculate. The whole staff and even some of the kids would gather around her each night to pray for her peace and protection, binding Satan and his demons from her life and their home.

Was life about to return to normal? Things seemed to be going so much better for Roxanne, but not for me. When I was in public, people seemed to be staring at me, and I could have sworn those same staring individuals appeared in various locations. I really didn't think it was my overstimulated imagination, but since life had been crazy and stressful for my wife and me, I wanted to be sure I wasn't experiencing a stress-induced paranoia. So I tried to remember faces to see if the same person or persons would be behind me or looking in my direction in different settings and different parts of the city.

One Saturday afternoon we visited Roxanne, and on a whim I asked her what she thought about people following me. I was half joking, but her response was very serious.

"Bill, I warned you what was going to happen," was her immediate answer. "You're being watched by people from the coven. They want *you* to lead them to *me*."

Now she was tearful as she asked, "Did anyone follow you today?"

I didn't think so and assured her that I thought she was safe. I made a note to myself to take a different route from then on to and from the center and home.

A few days later I was spinning records during my air shift when a staff member rushed into the studio, almost knocking the door off its hinges.

"There's been a bomb threat on the church!" he exclaimed. "We're evacuating. We all need to get out right now."

I programmed a long set of songs to make sure there would be no dead air and ran outside. We stood on the fringe of the parking lot, wondering what in the world was going on. I watched as police with impressive-looking German shepherds entered the building to begin the search. A couple of hours later they announced it had been a false alarm.

What was this about? A call had come in from someone saying there was a bomb in the church and they intended to blow up the building. Was this the members of Roxanne's coven trying to scare me into giving up the battle? There were more bomb threats against the church that year. Each time we had to follow the same procedure. We looked like a group of schoolchildren marching out the doors during a fire drill. We had to leave the building as the police searched the premises with their bomb-sniffing dogs.

I felt really bad that I might be the cause of such a hassle—and the consensus among some was that Roxanne was the reason this was happening. I was good-naturedly teased by church staff members and radio station workers from time to time. I was glad for their attempts to lighten the mood, but I wasn't laughing inside.

Maybe I was paranoid. And for good reason. I received other, more personal threats. Late-night calls at home. Messages that came through others. And always with the promise of pain or death.

I'll never forget the time I was working a live remote broadcast at an outdoor concert for one of the most popular Christian rock groups at the time in a nearby city within our listening area. After my airtime I was to host the concert and introduce the band. I arrived pumped up and looking forward to doing a great radio show and being part of a fabulous concert. While setting things up on the makeshift set we would use for the show, a police officer approached to tell me they had received what they considered a credible death threat and that he would be my security liaison. He told me that uniformed officers would monitor me closely. He wished me good luck and said to relax because they had things under control. Then he cautioned me to be very careful.

I had determined that I was not going to let Satan bully me. I was going to live my life the same way I had before the day Satan called. But I was scared. As I broadcast live, thousands formed lines to get in the concert early and grab the best seats for this general-admission event. Even as I laughed and joked I kept scanning the crowd, wondering if someone was actually going to try to hurt me.

My main worry was hosting the concert. That meant I would be on the stage in front of ten thousand people with the lights down low and a spotlight on me. That would be like painting a bull's-eye on my forehead. When the spotlight is pointed straight into your eyes, there is no way to see anyone in the audience. That made me feel even more vulnerable. But again, I was not going to give fear a foothold and allow it to gain control of my life. Nothing happened that night.

Fortunately, nothing happened as a result of any other threats made on my life. But how do you not take a death threat seriously, even if they all have proved to be false alarms? The fact that people are going to the trouble—and risk—of communicating hatred and violent intent is serious business.

In retrospect, it seems to me that the threats were somewhat parallel to confronting evil spirits in Jesus' name. There was an undoubtedly malignant presence that promised violence. But in the end, much of Satan's best work was a matter of talk designed to intimidate and defeat rather than actually cause physical harm.

I just wanted my life back. I appreciated Pastor Cliff's

commitment to maintain a ministry of battling evil spirits, but I wanted nothing to do with anything related to demons or witchcraft. That feeling has never changed through the years and is the reason I have been so reluctant to write a book about my experience.

One evening I received a call. It scared me almost as much as another death threat. A pastor from a church about an hour away had been given my name as an expert on dealing with witches and demons. He said there was a witch in their church building right now and they needed help. I politely declined. I told him that someone was mistaken about my being any kind of expert on the dark arts.

An expert on facing witches and demons? That was the last thing I wanted to try to be.

Then I began to feel bad about refusing to help people who needed assistance. I was in the same boat as them just a few months earlier. I called the pastor back and told him I was no expert but that I would be right over.

I called my younger brother Bob and asked if he would come along. He knew all that had been going on in my life, but I don't think he was convinced that everything I had said reflected reality. His response was similar to Dave's when I warned him about staying in our haunted house with us. But Bob not only agreed to ride with me, he was eager to do so.

We pulled up to the church and I told Bob we would just be there as prayer support and we didn't need to actually get involved. He thought that was a good idea. If I had had any question about Bob's faith and commitment, I would have told him to take the car somewhere for a cup of coffee, because this was serious business.

We walked into the building and I was escorted to where a seventeen-year-old girl was "in a world of hurt," said the woman who greeted us. There was a small crowd of people in the room, surrounding her and praying for her, but not sure what to do or how to effectively help her. The voice of a demon was speaking from her. Her eyes had rolled back so all we could see was the whites. It was an all-too-familiar scene. I was certain she was demon-possessed. Even though I was standing several feet from her, I raised a hand and prayed earnestly that the power of God and the blood of Jesus Christ would bind the demon or demons and cast all evil out of her life.

Before I knew what was happening, Bob and I were pushed to the front of the room and I looked up to find myself eye-to-eye with the teenage girl. This had not been my plan.

I was a young man in my twenties when all this happened, but I had been on the radio for years. As was and is common practice with announcers, I used a radio name on the air. Partly for obvious privacy reasons, but in many cases, including mine, it is just a little easier to say a shorter name on the air. So I never used my whole name in my radio work, but have always gone by Bill Scott, my first and middle names. So when the pastor called, he was looking for me as Bill Scott, not by my whole name as listed in the phone book. I'm pretty sure no one at that church knew my real last name.

So there I was, face-to-face with this young girl. Her eyes were cold and dark, boring into me with hatred. It wasn't her staring at me, it was the demon. Then a man's voice erupted from her and said, "Listen here, William ____, we are sick and tired of you causing us trouble!"

I am certain this girl didn't know me. I don't believe I had met anyone in the church before that day. Again, the pastor had asked for me by my on-air name. There was no one present who could have told her what my full name was.

I turned and looked at my brother. Bob wasn't sorting out the name thing. He was just terrified by the voice of the demon. Since he was my brother, I would definitely tell him "I told you so" later.

I looked back and the demon continued. "It's time we hurt you."

"You have no authority to harm me," I declared. "In Jesus' name, you must leave."

He wasn't listening and if he was, he wasn't ready to go.

"William, I have summoned people to go to your house and kill your wife. They are on their way now. We have had it with you."

I was terrified. But before I could react, the demon said something that literally almost made me wet my pants: "Where are you hiding Roxanne?"

This demon knew my last name and knew about Roxanne. He began to growl in the deep, resonant tone of a menacing animal, looking around the room through the girl's eyes to see whom he might devour.

"I see you have come alone," he said, turning back to me. "Your God has not come with you." He then launched into a very evil laugh.

I was distracted by the thought of my wife's safety when the demon, in the form of this petite teenager, grabbed me by the collar! I could feel an incredible strength pulling me closer! This wasn't a seventeen-year-old grabbing me. It was a supernatural power. In the background I could hear voices of alarm and screams as the demon pulled me closer until we were nose-to-nose. He looked me right in the eyes and said, "Do you know what you are dealing with? You are nothing more than a mere mortal."

I could see the girl's lips parting and her bared teeth. I thought to myself that I was about to die. I was no match for this evil spirit. My head cleared for just a second, and I remembered that Satan ruled by intimidation. Fear is Satan's tool to keep us using the power God has given us. I began to quote 1 John 4:4 in my head: *You are of God, little children, and have overcome them, because He who is in you is greater than he who is in the world.*

My courage was returning. This evil spirit's battle was not with me, so it didn't matter how powerful he was. He had to deal with God.

"You are wrong," I said. "I did not come alone. My God is with me. Your battle is with Him!"

The demon hissed and growled, and then spit in my face. I stood up straighter and pulled the girl's hands from my collar. I stepped back and said loudly enough for everyone in the room to hear: "My God is here, and it's Him you must deal with. In Jesus' name, come out of the girl and stand before Him. He meets you for battle in this very room."

There was dead silence. The demon didn't make a sound. Not one person was talking. They were probably holding their breath as they wondered if this battle would actually happen and they would witness a fight between a demon and the Creator of the universe.

The demon began to growl again, low and menacingly.

He stared into my eyes with all the hatred of the world. But God's Word was in me. I stood my ground, silently repeated, *He who is in you is greater than he who is in the world.*

The demon flinched and broke eye contact. Then he screamed with a wailing voice, "You know I cannot do that!" And again I heard the phrase from the very first night I spoke with Lacey on the phone: "One day I'll bow to the Lord and my lips will confess that Jesus is Lord—but today is not that day!"

I'm sure I didn't get the words quite right, but a passage from one of the Bible prophets was echoing through my mind and giving me tremendous confidence and comfort:

> *Do not fear;*
> *Zion, let not your hands be weak.*
> *The* LORD *your God in your midst,*
> *The Mighty One, will save;*
> *He will rejoice over you with gladness,*
> *He will quiet you with His love,*
> *He will rejoice over you with singing.* (Zephaniah 3:16–17)

The demon screamed as if tormented. It was as if he could read my mind or I had read the passage aloud. I can't tell you exactly how I knew, but I was sure the words of Scripture were responsible for driving him into fits.

We prayed with and over the girl for hours. I'll admit it felt good to have my brother at my side. In my humanness it had hurt me not to be believed by some of my close friends and even family members. Now Bob was praying against Satan as if it were the most natural thing in the world for a Christian to do. It was an amazing night. We heard the voices of many demons. But God's Word had imparted such a confidence to the whole group. I was no expert in facing the forces of evil. But I knew and believed with all my being the one thing, the only thing, that truly matters: God is more powerful than Satan. Satan and all his demons will one day bow before the Creator of the universe.

God gave me a supernatural peace that my wife was safe and I didn't need to worry. I was still concerned that the demon knew my full name, which had been unknown to everyone else present but my brother. And I wondered about the demon's rage over Roxanne's hiding place. Demons had been present there, and I had assumed it was only the witches that were blocked from knowing her whereabouts. Not everything added up in dealing with Roxanne and the demons of her life, but I knew my wife was okay.

I don't know why it seems to take more than one command for demons to leave when demons tremble at the name of Jesus. Maybe this happens only when there are multiple demons, or demons coupled with severe psychological disorders like schizophrenia or multiple personality disorder (MPD). But finally the demonic activity stopped. The young girl spoke now. She told everyone in the room that she was part of a witches' coven and desperately needed help. A young couple who had prayed with us throughout the night invited her home with them while they worked on finding her a place to get help. This alarmed me. I had just gotten my own house clean from

Roxanne's time with us. I took them aside and encouraged them to be very careful, especially about the objects they allowed this girl to bring inside their home and to pray against Satan every morning and night.

I didn't want to scare them, but I realized they needed to be scared. So I was blunt with my words and offered no assurance to them that the horror they had just witnessed was over.

My brother didn't say a word on the drive home. He was stunned by what he saw. I knew it would take some time for him to sort out what he had experienced and that we could talk later.

Once home, I told my wife about the night. We just looked at each other in amazement. Somehow we had entered a battle that we still didn't fully comprehend—and to which we didn't know if there would ever be an end.

What I did know was that I was committed to fighting this battle with the Lord's strength and power. I knew that I could not give up. I felt that Satan was trying to get me to back down through all these threats and ongoing demonic encounters. My stubbornness is not always a good trait, but in a positive light, it means I am not a quitter.

The next morning I received a call from the couple who had taken this young girl home. I asked how their night went. They said it was a bizarre and wild evening and they didn't get a lot of sleep. I could understand fully. I knew how things were when you entered this kind of battle. They weren't farmers but lived out in the country. During the night cows from neighboring properties circled the house and began to head-butt their walls. I thought I couldn't be surprised by anything else related to what I had been going through, but this revelation was the strongest yet.

Throughout the week the couple would sometimes put me on the phone to talk with the young girl. I was trying so hard not to get involved. My encounters with Roxanne were all I could handle. But I wouldn't say no to someone in need. The girl began calling a couple of times a day. The talks were all upbeat and positive. She seemed to be doing fine. She told me the family she was living with was awesome, and she really appreciated the opportunity to get a fresh start. I was so glad to hear this.

Toward the end of the week the girl called asking if I would come to her baptism service on Sunday. That was exciting. Unfortunately, I had a previous engagement booked. I told her how happy I was for her but that I couldn't make it. She called a couple more times that day—and the next—asking me to change my plans and then begging me to attend the baptism.

My first thoughts were that her eagerness and persistence were positive signs, but after a few more calls on the third day, things began to feel wrong. Strange, but I didn't feel peace about her baptism.

On the Friday before the service, she called one last time asking if I would attend. Once again I told her I couldn't make it but wished her God's very best.

"I hate you, Bill Scott!" she screamed.

"I hate you," she said again, anger oozing from her words. "Now I cannot stay in this home any longer. You cast too many demons out of me. I am growing too weak to stay with this family."

My mind was reeling. She was a plant, too? She showed up at the church not for help but to harm?

"In Jesus' name, why are you there?" I asked.

"I was sent to kill you," she said, her words chilling me to the core. "That is the only reason I wanted you at the baptism service. That's where we planned it."

"In Jesus' name, what do you want with me?" I demanded.

"You know what we want, Bill." It was no longer her voice but that of a demon. "We want Roxanne back, and you need to bring her to us." The phone went dead.

I talked to the couple that night and several more times in the days ahead. Apparently, after slamming the phone down, she stormed out of the house. They never saw her again.

After the witch—or demon—hung up on me, I just sat at my office desk, thinking about the conversation and this encounter with a second witch filled with demons.

If I had gone to the baptism service, would there really have been an attempt on my life, or was this another false alarm? When these troubled young women came to us, was any part of them truly seeking help? When she said she was growing too weak to stay in the home, was it because the power of the gospel was getting to her?

I had talked to Roxanne earlier in the week. She had said she was doing great. Was she still part of a plot to do harm, or had she really become a new person in Christ?

CHAPTER 15

Will This Ever Stop?

When was all of this going to stop? The demons, witches, covens, death threats, bomb threats, people following me, late-night calls. I didn't ask for any of this. I was just trying to help Roxanne, who said she wanted to receive Jesus into her life and escape her coven. My life had been turned upside down.

A few close friends who had been observing this over the last couple of months were amazed at the level of spiritual activity surrounding me. I just couldn't seem to get away from it all. It was as if I had become a magnet for anyone who had spiritual warfare going on in their life.

My father called me late one night. We started talking about the journey I had been on for the last couple of months. He wasn't sure what to think, and he didn't have any new advice other than for me to continue to rely on God. But I could tell there was something else he wanted to talk about. Finally I asked, "Dad, something's on your mind. What do you really want to talk about?"

He admitted there was a young woman in his church who seemed to be struggling with demonic influences. He asked if I would meet with her and just pray with her. I desperately wanted to say no. I wanted to keep things with my dad on the sane side of my life. But I couldn't legitimately come up with a reason to refuse him; after all, he was my father.

A couple of days later I drove down to his church with a couple of my closest friends. We met with the woman in his office to talk and pray. I didn't want to assume that she was demon-possessed. Many of us struggle with the hurts and troubles of life, but without the harassments of demons. From the few things my dad had described, though, I was afraid she might be demon-possessed.

No sooner had we sat down at the small table than she started rolling her eyes with a glazed expression. The group of friends who traveled with me were now experienced in satanic battle. It wasn't that they weren't shocked each time or afraid. They just knew the various ways Satan would begin his attack. I looked at my dad. But to our surprise, the girl's behavior didn't get any worse.

However, things kept happening with this young lady that went far beyond the realm of normal. My dad called again and asked if this girl could come and meet with us in our town. This time a full display of satanic activity was seen. We were cursed at and taunted. We were told we were powerless and helpless. The pattern always seemed to be the same. We would fall for the same tricks of intimidation every time and lose heart, and then through the power of God's Word and the help of the Holy Spirit, we would regain our courage to rebuke and cast out demons in Jesus' name. I've talked to several other people engaged in spiritual warfare against demons through the years, and in most cases, it seems most often there is a moment when a single demon is cast out and the possessed person experiences an immediate spiritual healing.

This was just not the case for me and my spiritual warrior friends. We had always cast out multiple demons over prolonged periods of time. Sometimes in one evening, sometimes over weeks. That was the same with this woman in my dad's church. I should have asked him how long she had been attending, and I might have realized sooner we were dealing with the same situation as the witch who had disappeared. She wasn't there to receive help. She was there to press us for the location of Roxanne.

We met with this young woman a number of times over a three-week period. We had many victories, but never the victory where she was free from evil spirits.

In one encounter a demon spoke from her and said he was a spirit of nicotine. Even though I think cigarette smoking is a bad habit and a foolish health risk, I have never considered it a sin or barrier to heaven. My dad and many others disagree with me and I may be wrong, but I have never been able to tell someone it is a sin. I will confess, though, that every time the demon spoke, we smelled cigarette smoke in the air.

After three weeks and little progress, we talked it over as a group and decided to not continue seeing her. I think we had come to realize that she had a hidden agenda. We wondered if she had been sent as a distraction to keep us from praying as much for Roxanne's deliverance.

My dad had had enough of her, too, and agreed. But just as when I told the young witch I couldn't attend her baptism service the first time, this woman was not happy and begged us to keep meeting with her.

She somehow got my home phone number. One night she called late to let me know again how upset she was that we had stopped meeting with her and how this was proof that the love of God was not inside us. I respectfully told her that I was not going to have this argument with her again. Then for the first time on the phone, the demons began to speak through her. I had been there and done that. I was just not going to put up with it on this night.

"I'm going to hang up now," I said into the mouthpiece.

"I'll just call back," the demon answered.

"Then I'll disconnect the phone," I said.

We were starting to sound like two kids arguing on the playground.

"Go ahead and disconnect the phone," he said with an evil laugh. "I can still make it ring!"

Not only did he get in the last word, but I think he could have actually done it.

I wondered again, *Will this ever stop?* The answer didn't take long in coming.

A few days later I was at the radio station when I received a phone call from the front desk. Michelle, the receptionist, said her eleven-year-old son, Matthew, was at home and something bad was happening to him.

"Did he have an accident?" I asked.

"No, it's the kind of stuff you've been dealing with," she said.

I wanted to ask her what kind of "stuff" she meant, but I had an eerie feeling that I already knew.

Michelle asked me to pray and said she would call if needed. I prayed for both her and Matt. About thirty minutes later she called me from home. She was in tears. She said that Matt was rolling on the floor, foaming at the mouth, and a strange voice was coming from him.

"Something just told me Matt belongs to them," Michelle said through sobs. "Can I bring Matthew to you so you can pray over him?"

"If it's safe to drive with him, bring Matt to the radio studio and we can all pray for him."

Beyond the sinking feeling that my involvement in demon-related activities was never going to end—I had never signed up to be a minister of exorcism—this situation was confusing. From everything I had seen and heard, Matt was a good kid. A great kid. I knew him from church and other activities and couldn't figure out how this happy young boy from a great family could have gotten mixed up in evil spirits.

Michelle and Matt arrived in no time. He looked frightened and confused. I had the sense that he had no idea what was happening to him. He wasn't in the thralls of a demonic episode, and I wondered if Michelle had gotten this all wrong. A small group, most of whom had dealt with Roxanne, gathered in my office. Matt just sat in a chair across from me, saying very little unless I asked him a specific question, such as "Has everything been going okay at school?" or "Has anything strange been happening to you lately?"

He'd just nod or give one-word or short-sentence responses.

Then his eyes began to change. I had seen that look before. I could see in his eyes that there was indeed something there. At that moment a demon began to speak through Matt. After all I had experienced, I'm not sure why I was amazed, but I was. The voice was angry.

"He is ours. We have been in his family for generations, and he is ours."

I looked over at Michelle. Her eyes were clenched shut tightly and she was deep in prayer.

Then the demon said, "He'll be a drunk and a drug addict because he is ours. We have been here for generations, and we are not going to leave."

A lot has been said about "generational sin" in some church circles. The idea is that certain sins are passed down from one generation to the next until the chain is broken. Some scientists talk about certain tendencies and inclinations, both physiological and psychological, being a function of genetics. I am sure there is much we can learn from both lines of thought. But I also know what the prophet Ezekiel said in speaking for God:

> You say, "Why should the son not bear the guilt of the father?" Because the son has done what is lawful and right, and has kept all My statutes and observed them, he shall surely live. The soul who sins shall die. The son shall not bear the guilt of the father, nor the father bear the guilt of the son. The righteousness of the righteous shall be upon himself, and the wickedness of the wicked shall be upon himself. (Ezekiel 18:19–20)

So I wasn't going to believe that demons had some binding right of ownership over this boy. I did not believe for a second that they could not be made to leave in the name of Jesus.

I began to ask Matt questions.

"Matt, do you have any unforgiveness in your life?" His answer was no.

"Are you angry?" No.

"Have you been involved in anything weird and scary—anything on TV or some games?" No.

Finally Michelle interrupted and said, "I have the unforgiveness in my life."

We all looked at her in shock.

She told us she was angry because her mom was a drunk and as a child she had to raise her brothers and sisters as if she were their mother. She did all the housework and cooked meals because her mom was out drinking or passed out in her bedroom.

Her mom had become a Christian and was doing fine now, which made Michelle feel guilty over her feelings of resentment and unforgiveness toward her mom.

Could the demons lay claim to her son through her unforgiveness? Again, I'm no theologian, but my response would be no. I've already noted the passage in Ezekiel that is one of the clearest Old Testament expressions of what is understood throughout the New Testament: personal accountability.

But now was not the time to sort everything out. I simply asked Michelle, "Do you want to forgive your mom?"

With tears streaming down her face, she said yes. We forgot about Matt for just a second and prayed with Michelle as she asked God to give her the grace and power to do what she had not previously wanted to do. She prayed a beautiful prayer for and of forgiveness. All I could add at the end was a short prayer that God would bless and protect Michelle's family.

And then a miracle happened. As Michelle prayed to forgive her mom, Matthew returned 100 percent to a happy, vibrant young boy. And we hadn't even prayed to cast the demons out. They were gone.

He asked his mom why they were at her office. When had they come over to where she worked? I'm sure his mom said something; I just don't recall. But I'm glad he didn't ask me. I was so stunned I doubt I could have given an intelligent answer.

More than twenty years later, Matt still remembers that day when his family was delivered from a curse—though not the drive over to the church—and since then there has never been another recurrence of demonic activity in his life.

In some ways this experience is the most difficult for me to explain. Was Matt possessed? Or were there demons that had access to the home and some permission to be there through Michelle's unforgiveness and family tree—not unlike the paraphernalia from Roxanne's past—but more as an oppressive presence than a possessive force? He appeared to be possessed, and I believe a demon was present. I won't make any claims beyond that, but I would note that Michelle was a single mom who was Matt's "spiritual covering," and I believe she had left the door open in some way that made her son vulnerable.

It seemed that everywhere I turned, I was dealing with some expression of the occult, demons, or witchcraft. This could just have been a season of intense demonic activity because things like this had never happened to me before, and they have not happened since. But at the time I was a magnet for spiritual warfare.

I even had a young man on death row call in as a guest on my show. This young man, now a Christian, was so obsessed with the game Dungeons and Dragons that his role-playing turned to satanic involvement. At the age of sixteen he shot and killed his mom and his dad. He was later executed, but like the thief on the cross next to Jesus who came to believe he was the Christ, he, too, went on to live in paradise at his death. Demon-free.

Because of death threats on my life, I met with a few police officers over the next year who claimed that one of the dirty secrets of law enforcement was the amount of crime related to satanic activity and coven rituals that is never reported that way. I continue to hear the same report to varying degrees.

Despite more involvement in ministry against dark forces than I could ever have imagined, the good news was that at home things were quiet for almost a year. No demonic activity. The lights turned on or off only when the switch was flipped. That was good enough for me.

Roxanne had been gone from our home for almost nine months when that tranquillity was shattered. In the middle of one night, my wife sat straight up in bed and screamed. I awoke from a dead sleep and jumped out of bed. Bleary-eyed, I looked around, trying to figure out what in the world was going on.

I looked over at her and she said, "Someone was in our room."

I checked all the doors and windows in the house and asked her what she'd seen—and if it could have been a repeat of what we went through with Roxanne.

She shook her head vigorously and said, "No, it was a man, and he was sitting on the edge of our bed staring at us."

She went on to describe him in great detail. There was neither explanation nor evidence for this. We talked about it into the early morning hours, went back to sleep, and then resumed the conversation the next day. I had come to the conclusion that she'd just had a very vivid, lifelike dream. So I wasn't worried about it when we went to bed the next night. That was, until she experienced a repeat performance—and this became a regular nightly occurrence.

She was convinced she saw people walking down the hall or sitting in our bedroom. They would disappear when we turned on the lights. But she could still describe them in great detail. I wasn't seeing the people, and I couldn't understand what was happening because things had been so peaceful for almost nine months.

I did not think for one moment that my wife was crazy—although the past year had beaten us both up emotionally. But we didn't know what to do next. We needed relief. Should we have our home anointed again? Did we need to go to counseling together?

Right or wrong, I didn't feel that I could tell friends and colleagues the strange occurrences in our home had begun again. Everyone had been faithful to and supportive of us, but I didn't want to test the bounds of their patience and understanding.

People continued to ask me to help them with evil spirits—but here I was, once again back at the point where I couldn't even take care of my own household.

Through the grapevine I heard about a minister who had dealt with many occult practices because his community was abnormally active in alternative religions and practices. I called to ask for help and he enthusiastically agreed to meet with my wife and me. We met him in his office and told the whole story, beginning with the call from Lacey and on up to the night before, when once again my wife had seen people watching us.

Without blinking an eye he said, "These are real people in your home, and they are watching you."

"If they are real people, then where do they go when we turn on the lights?" I challenged.

"Not many people believe it," he said, "but there is such a thing as soul travel, where a person leaves his or her human body and travels to other places to observe things and even interact. All that time, the human body is back where it was left. Maybe in bed sleeping. Maybe at a satanic ritual. From all you've told me, people from Roxanne's coven are traveling to your home. This is why your wife can describe in detail what they are wearing. She can really see these people and they can see her as well."

"What do we do?" I asked.

"What have you tried so far?"

"We've asked that these demons be cast from our house in Jesus' name," I answered.

"But you are not dealing with spirits; these are real people," he answered.

"So there's nothing we can do?" we both nearly shouted in unison.

It seemed he was about to laugh at us, but then he got very serious. "Just pray more specifically. You don't need to cast out demons. You simply need to ask God to bind any satanic powers that provide these people with access to your home. And you already know to do everything in the name of Jesus."

We prayed together, and my wife and I started the drive home. On one hand, we felt we had received the help we needed to see peace restored in our home. On the other hand, we felt violated at the thought that real people had been watching us in our home. My home had been robbed once before, but I didn't have that feeling of violation that is a common emotion from victims. This time I did. And this was an over-the-top invasion, creepy, like we had been secretly videotaped.

We didn't have time to feel too sorry for ourselves. We were eager to get home to pray over our home and bind this satanic practice. We continued to pray for protection on a daily basis before going to bed. The good news was, it stopped. We didn't see anything or anyone in our home from that point forward.

Once again, things were quiet in the house. If you have a peaceful home, I cannot encourage you strongly enough to never take it for granted. It was a relief and joy to come home to an oasis of peace. Unfortunately for us, it seemed that each time we would think we had reached the end of this long, arduous, battle-filled journey, something else terrifying or strange happened. That proved to be the case once again. It was late one evening and I was about to go to sleep. I was lying in bed with the lights out, stretching and yawning, my wife already fast asleep. There it was. Again. I felt an evil presence! This hadn't happened in such a long time, how could it be?

But something was different this time. I lay still and took stock. I realized that the evil presence I felt was coming from outside the house, not inside. This almost made me feel better, but then I became very aware that this evil presence was huge. This was far more evil than I had dealt with in the past. Was it a person or a demon? I still had no idea. I just knew there was a threatening, malignant evil presence outside our house, and it wanted in.

God spoke to me, in a loud, commanding voice: *Start praying right now. If you stop, you and your wife will die tonight.*

Without a second's hesitation I began praying for protection in the name of Jesus in as many ways as I knew how. This went on for hours. When I would start to get sleepy and stop, I would immediately be awakened by an overwhelming feeling that the evil presence was drawing closer and growing heavier, denser—like a dark cloud that would suffocate not just me, but the whole house. My breathing was labored. I would start praying with all the fervor and faith I could muster again. It might be fifteen minutes or it might be an hour, but invariably I would tire again and my words would come to a stop, and then the presence would grow closer. I don't know how many times this cycle was repeated, but I just knew I couldn't fall asleep or stop praying.

What was outside my home? Would we really have died if I had stopped praying? I believe to this very day the answer is yes.

I looked at the clock at 4:00 a.m. I was dead tired. By this time all I could pray was, "Jesus, Jesus, Jesus!" That was all I had left inside me. Despite standing up and walking around, I knew I was going to fall asleep. In desperation I asked the Lord if He would impress on other people to pray for us so I could go to sleep. Amazingly, I felt a real peace about that. I was asleep in just minutes.

I awoke a little rested and a lot relieved. We were alive. My first thought was that someone had prayed for us.

While getting ready for work and pouring coffee, I told my wife about the all-night ordeal and we agreed to talk later. I was running late so I dashed out the door for work.

I walked into the radio station for our weekly staff meeting. There was the usual chitchat before we got started. Then one of the staffers said to the group, "I am so tired. I can't believe I woke up at four in the morning."

Did I just hear what I thought I'd heard?

"I just felt that I should pray for someone because they were in grave danger. I have no idea who it was, what danger they were in, or why God asked me to pray. But I actually prayed until I heard the alarm go off."

I opened my mouth to thank her, when another lady said, "That is really weird. I woke up at 4:00 a.m., too. And I had the same feeling I should be praying for someone's safety."

I was awestruck. I felt thankful to God for His goodness—and the goodness of His people. I spoke up and told them that it was my wife and I they had been praying for. I shared the story of the night before, and our staff meeting turned into a prayer meeting instead.

If you feel God has impressed on your heart to pray for someone in need—even if you don't know that person's name or what they look like—pray! You may not know until you meet Jesus in glory what you accomplished, but your prayers matter and make a difference. I love the words of James on the power of prayer: "The effective, fervent prayer of a righteous man avails much" (James 5:16).

I don't know what was outside my home. I do know the evil presence was real and that it was a deeper level of evil than I had felt up to that point. I began to think about the previous year—how much evil I had seen and yet how much power I had seen in God. I wondered again if this would ever end. Was there a way out of this diabolical maze that I found myself living in? I wanted to help people, but it was emotionally overwhelming to live like this. I had thought once Roxanne went to the ministry center to get help, our part in her story was over and life would return to normal.

After everything we had been through, we could not imagine anything getting much worse.

CHAPTER 16

Roxanne Returns

The apostle Paul encourages us to reach out to those who are lost in sin: "Brethren, if a man is overtaken in any trespass, you who are spiritual restore such a one in a spirit of gentleness, considering yourself lest you also be tempted" (Gal. 6:1).

Don't miss Paul's warning at the end of the verse. Yes, we are to reach out to those who are lost—but we need to guard our own hearts and souls as well. On a personal level, this chapter is the most painful to write. I didn't go off the deep end and get mixed up in a life of sin and debauchery. But I'm not pleased and proud of the way I was thinking, not just in terms of my own spiritual safety, but in terms of the safety of those closest to me.

Roxanne had been at the group home for about a year, and it was time for her to graduate. Graduation is always an exciting time. So why wasn't I excited?

My wife, friends, and I had visited Roxanne all year, usually on Saturday afternoons. We were her only "family," so we felt it was important to support her. She was doing well in so many ways. But she was not free from evil spirits. There were no more major episodes at the home, but when I sat down to chat with her, there were numerous times when a normal conversation would be interrupted by a variety of voices, from little kids to old men. The common complaint was that no one from her coven could find her. I thank God for that supernatural protection. But did it really matter when there was still demonic activity going on inside her?

Shortly before her graduation, a group of us went to visit Roxanne. It was a beautiful summer day. As I was sitting at a picnic table and talking with Roxanne, she got this really weird look in her eyes. I had seen it so many times before, I thought I knew what was coming. But then I realized something was different. I was feeling an evil presence I had never felt before. And this time it was in broad daylight. Roxanne's eyes seemed to physically morph until they looked like a snake's eyes—little slits. She began swaying back and forth with her body the way a cobra would if coiled up and preparing to strike. Roxanne's appearance and movements were the creepiest thing I have ever experienced or seen.

I just stared at her as if under a spell. The evil was suffocating. All the evil I had felt and experienced up to this point was dwarfed by what was in front of me. What was going on? Why was this happening? Where was everyone else?

The demon spoke to me in a low, quiet, confident voice: "You found me."

Pastor Cliff had told me there would be no doubt when I met Abaddon. I was meeting Abaddon.

I had been terrified in the past. I had thought I was seeing demons face-to-face at other times. But this went deeper. Even though the body of Roxanne was in front of me, still swaying back and forth, it was as if all humanity had been stripped away and I was now in the presence of evil in its essence. The dark, evil slits held me in their gaze as if the snake were attempting to put me in a trance before it struck.

If the name Abaddon seems familiar to you, perhaps it's because you've read it in Scripture. In speaking of the forces of evil, we find in Revelation 9:11 these words: "They had as king over them the angel of the bottomless pit, whose name in Hebrew is Abaddon, but in Greek he has the name Apollyon."

I had looked up the meaning of *Abaddon*, and a literal translation is "destroyer." I thought of Roxanne's notebook that listed ten years of contacts with ministries, churches, and Christian couples. I had spoken to many of them. There was a littered trail of church splits, ministries closing, ministers defrocked, and couples going through divorce. The name Destroyer was very apt.

Was I in the presence of Satan himself? If not, I was sure I was looking at a presence very close to him. But why Roxanne? And why me?

"Roxanne is mine," he said quietly, slowly, and clearly, so I wouldn't miss a single word. "You will never free her. Much better people than you have tried to cast me out, and it hasn't happened yet. Be assured I'll kill her before you ever get me to leave her. I will not leave. You have no idea what you are dealing with."

Abaddon never spoke to me again. He said enough to last a lifetime.

I had the power of God inside me, but in my humanness, I was in way over my head. Some demons will leave only through prayer and fasting and over time. I simply was not able to confront this demon; it wasn't the time or place. All I said was, "I rebuke you in Jesus' name."

His only response was silence.

I prayed as hard as I could, my lips moving, but no sound came out. I don't know if I stayed there face-to-face with Roxanne for five minutes or five seconds. But at some point the spell passed and she was Roxanne again. I jumped up from the picnic table and went to where my friends were. No one seemed to have noticed anything.

On the drive home I told everyone what had happened and how I had been nearly frozen in time and space. After a few minutes of silence we talked things over. The biggest concern was that Roxanne had come so far, but as soon as she graduated she was going to be taken to a new location by Abaddon before she could truly be free of the demonic strongholds in her life.

But what could we do? Where was a safe place she could stay? If it came down to one demon controlling her, even if he was a general in Satan's army, surely we could gather people of strong faith to see this demon cast out. We didn't come up with a plan at that point, but the conversation continued over the next two weeks before graduation.

After numerous talks with my wife, I convinced her—and myself—to allow Roxanne to live with us. This was against my wife's and friends' better judgment. I was so focused on the thought that the final battle and ultimate victory for Roxanne were at hand that I didn't listen and wasn't using good judgment. The decision was that she could stay for a month, possibly two. Enough time to get a job, buy a car, and get on her own feet—and be free from Abaddon.

We picked up Roxanne at the center on graduation day. I was proud of her, almost like a father would be when his child graduated from high school. I appropriately felt this was a real victory, that we had actually accomplished something.

In addition to feeling proud of Roxanne, I felt sorry for her. She was alone in the world. I couldn't bear the thought of her fighting the battle without the help of loving friends. As Christians we are called to be compassionate and loving. But I would caution you at this point that some people will use your compassion against you. We are to consider our own families' needs and spiritual well-being when ministering to others.

Roxanne was happy to be going home with us. The mood was very light in the car. No problems on the drive, just a happy Roxanne in the backseat. We pulled into the driveway and helped Roxanne bring in her stuff so she could get situated in our guest bedroom. I remember thinking, *Lord, help us. This just has to go much better than the first time.*

And the first couple of days seemed to pass quickly and with no incidents. I let a glimmer of hope seep into my heart and mind. Could the fight be over? Had we finally succeeded in the battle of good versus evil?

But my dreams were crushed just a few days later. It was dinnertime, and the three of us were sitting at the kitchen table talking about mundane things, getting ready to eat. I looked up only to see that look in Roxanne's eyes again.

"Because of you," a demon growled at me, "we are going to kill Roxanne. She is no longer hidden and safe. And you will be responsible for her death. You should have listened."

I could see he was tormenting Roxanne just by the way

her body was moving and twisting at the dinner table. She was in obvious pain.

"Leave me alone, in Jesus' name," Roxanne screamed, trying to take control. I was amazed and pleased at the new person she was becoming. But then she was lifted out of her chair and thrown several feet from the table. It was like someone picked her up and tossed her like a rag doll. She was physically okay, but she was stunned. So were we. Before we could help her up, she stood up on her own and sat back down at the table.

"I guess that really made him mad," she said in a quiet voice. Evidently we had gotten too used to the bizarre activities of the past year because, unlike most families, we simply picked up our forks and resumed eating as if nothing had happened.

I didn't confront this particular demon because I had decided beforehand that I was not going to do this in our home. My plan was that we would go to the church with a group of friends to pray for Roxanne's deliverance from the spiritual stronghold Abaddon had on her.

I'm sure I was being more than a little naive. If the demons decided to appear while Roxanne was at our house, that's where the warfare would take place. But gratefully, for the most part, the battles were not waged in our house. I believe the prayers of anointing and protection made all the difference this time—and with Roxanne's sincere desire to follow Christ, there were fewer open doors for the demons to access our home.

I knew the time had come for a showdown. A few nights later I arranged for a group of friends to meet us in the prayer room at the church. Roxanne was eager for this to happen as well, just another indicator of how far she had come.

We met a little later in the evening than I wanted to in order to accommodate everyone's schedule. We sat in a circle and began to pray for Roxanne's complete deliverance, including the expulsion of Abaddon.

The fireworks began almost immediately. The demons growled, yelled profanities, cursed us, blasphemed against God, and told us they were going to kill Roxanne if we didn't stop. We prayed on with all the confidence we could muster.

Demons were cast out. But as always seemed to be the case with Roxanne, more took their place. How many demons could live in one person? Were they leaving and the same ones coming back or was there a never-ending flow of new demons? How could we make them all leave at once? If there was more than one personality inside Roxanne, how could we make every demon inhabiting every personality leave at the same time?

I began to read Scripture out loud. One pastor had told me to just sit down and read the Bible in order to drive some demons out. Although I knew God's Word made demons feel uncomfortable, I wasn't sure if it made them leave. But I didn't know what else to do, so I began to read. Halfway through reading a chapter from the Bible the demon interrupted me, saying, "You missed a word. If you cannot read it right, don't read it at all. Would you like me to finish the chapter?"

I was once again amazed. Apparently not only did demons believe there is one God and tremble, they knew Scripture, too.

We continued to battle for Roxanne, this time through

prayer. At one point she started speaking German. Someone in the group was of German heritage and knew German well enough to understand much of what was being said. She was amazed at what was coming from Roxanne's mouth. She told us the demon said it had been in Roxanne's family for generations, going all the way back to the World War. The demon didn't specify whether it was WWI or WWII, but it didn't matter how many generations it had been there. In Jesus' name it had no choice but to leave. And it did. I was surprised to find out later that Roxanne didn't know any German herself.

She continued to live with us even after she found a job. She wasn't making much money but needed to build a small reserve of money before she moved into her own apartment. We were able to sell her old car and help her buy the most basic transportation. So life was fairly uneventful with Roxanne becoming more independent and away from the house most days. Every once in a while spiritual activity would flare up, but I would prayerfully ignore whatever was being done or said to wait for the right time to engage in spiritual warfare. I was determined that we would choose the times and places to pray with and over Roxanne so that it would be on our timetable, not Satan's.

Overall, it seemed as though Roxanne's life was finally coming together. However, she still had some very powerful demons directing her life.

CHAPTER 17

Space Travel and the Road Trip

It was just another day at the radio station, and all seemed to be going well. It was less stressful knowing Roxanne was working as well and not spending the whole day at our home.

I took a call, and for the first time in a year it was the voice of a demon on the phone. As I've said, I recorded a number of conversations with demons. Ten seconds was about the limit of what people could take before begging me to turn off the machine, often with a shout. Many people were moved to tears within seconds. Everyone that heard even a snippet was convinced the voice they heard was that of a demon. That was the kind of voice on the line now.

"We want Roxanne back," it said. "Stop getting involved."

I quickly rebuked the voice in Jesus' name and hung up. Then my next request line started ringing. It was the same demon again. I hung up. Then all my lines lit up at once. As I answered each one it said, "It's me, it's me, it's me, it's me, it's me," on all ten lines.

Then the demon said, "We watch you all the time. I can see your pretty red shirt right now."

That terrified me. I was indeed wearing a red shirt and

was horrified to think that demons were actually watching me at this moment. Then suddenly the calls stopped.

My wife and I no longer knew what to do. We could not get the demons out of Roxanne's life. It seemed the more we tried and fought, the more we had to deal with. Roxanne's demon possession just wasn't going away.

Again I called pastors, authors, speakers, and laypeople with a ministry in the area of the occult and demon possession all over the country. No one was able to give me a satisfactory answer to why Roxanne could not be free from the demons that plagued her life. But I kept calling. Someone somewhere had to have an answer. We then took Roxanne to a counselor. I couldn't imagine this professional had training for what she was about to face, but Roxanne's issues seemed to be both spiritual and psychological. Every Monday I would drive Roxanne to her appointment. I was concerned she would find reasons to miss sessions if she had to drive herself. The sessions were private, so I didn't know what went on for the fifty minutes they met each week. From my perspective, not much was changing. I have a lot of confidence in professional counseling, especially Christian counseling, since spiritual and psychological issues are often intertwined. But I was also confident Roxanne was not the regular client. All this time Roxanne continued to deal with one demon after another with seemingly no relief.

My wife and I would also take Roxanne to the radio station when I did my Saturday night show, which was geared toward teenagers. Though in her mid-thirties she really liked the show. We were trying to expose her to as much of God's Word and commonsense teaching as we could.

I was preparing for my show one Saturday night. There were four or five staffers and volunteers already at the station. I had a good team of people who worked on my Saturday night show. I was in the production room by myself working on some elements for the program I would air that night. Things seemed to be pretty normal. All of a sudden the door flew wide open. Roxanne stepped in and shut the door behind her. I didn't think anything of it and barely looked up. Now, keep in mind our studios were 100 percent soundproof. You could be just outside the door, but if someone was screaming in the studio, you couldn't hear them.

I still had my head down, busy at work, thinking that Roxanne probably had a question. After she didn't say anything for a moment or two, I looked up. There it was. That look in her eyes. I could see the anger and hatred building. The voice of a demon erupted from her mouth. I looked out the window and saw people milling around outside the studio, but no one was looking over to see what was going on. They couldn't hear anything.

I felt I was in danger and stood up to walk over to the door. She blocked my path. I walked around her and reached for the handle and turned and pulled it. She pushed against the door to keep it shut. I pulled harder. It didn't budge. I pulled as hard as I could and put my entire weight into the effort. Nothing.

With amazing quickness and supernatural strength, Roxanne grabbed me by the collar and lifted me off my feet. This wasn't Roxanne. It was the demon. I was terrified.

The demon drew me close to Roxanne's face and said, "I am so sick of you! I'm not going to kill Roxanne, I'm going to kill you!"

I couldn't believe no one was looking over to see what was happening to me. Then Roxanne made a fist with her other hand and pulled back her arm.

I looked again through the glass, hoping to see some-one looking my way. No one was. I had to do some-thing, and I had to do something quick. I was no match for the strength of this demon. I had not been in a fist-fight since grade school. But even if I had been trained to fight in mixed martial arts, I was going to lose. I then did the only thing I could think of. I closed my eyes and be-gan to pray. I knew that only God Himself could prevent me from being hurt seriously or even killed. I prayed the following prayer, which I remember word for word even today: "Lord, I need Your help. Please send Your angels to come and fight on my behalf. Please take care of this demon for me."

Instantly the demon released me, and I was standing on my own two feet. I didn't feel safe yet. I was waiting for impact. Nothing happened. My eyes were still closed, but I could hear the demon growling somewhere close to me.

I slowly opened my eyes, and, to my surprise, Roxanne was pinned against the wall five feet from me. Her arms were spread to either side of her, pressed hard against the wall. Her feet were barely touching the floor. Some force was pushing Roxanne against the wall and holding her in place.

The demon started screaming, "Let go of me!" He would look at his right hand and then his left hand and yell again, "Let go of me now!"

I was dumbfounded. My prayer worked. God had sent angels to fight this demon for me. I quickly opened the studio door and called for my friends and colleagues to come in and look at what was happening. They looked at Roxanne, who was still not Roxanne but the demon, pinned against the wall. I quickly told them what had happened, and we began to rebuke the demons that tortured Roxanne's life once again.

I don't know why I was surprised that God came to my rescue, but I was. He promises to do that throughout the Bible. But to actually see it happen right in front of you, to experience it in such dramatic form, is awe-inspiring.

Monday came, and it was time to take Roxanne to the counselor. I called ahead and asked if she thought it would be helpful to have a joint session that included me. She agreed that it would be.

I had shared with her before the first session that Roxanne had demons. Like the director and staff at the group home, she was polite but ignored me. I was pretty sure she didn't believe my diagnosis. I told her again on the phone what I thought was going on.

We were invited into the office and the three of us sat down. I began to share with the counselor that Roxanne really did have demons. Some would say that I was planting thoughts in her head and creating false memories and harmful expectations. But Roxanne had lived this stuff. She wanted to be free. She was at a place of honesty and candor in her life.

As I shared a few recent stories so the counselor would understand the level of spiritual activity we were dealing with, Roxanne looked at her and then me and nodded her head in agreement with what I was saying. I wondered if she felt the counselor wasn't listening to her. She almost had a smug "I told you so" look on her face when she looked at the counselor.

The counselor began to tell me in very general terms what she thought was going on with Roxanne but then stopped midsentence. We could all feel the presence of evil in the office. She stared at me with a look of shock. We both looked at Roxanne, whose eyes had changed. When Roxanne screamed obscenities at the counselor, I thought she was going to tumble backward in her chair. Then Roxanne started growling like a wild animal. I saw a look of terror in the counselor's eyes. She was speechless. Her years of education had not prepared her for an experience like this.

I looked carefully at Roxanne and she was back, unaware of the drama that had unfolded just seconds before. We never went back to that counselor again. But we still needed answers. We were going around in circles. I could not fight these demons and witches for the rest of my life. I wasn't sure I had another day of battle in me.

At some point we needed victory so Roxanne could be free from the evil forces at work inside her. She seemed like such a sweet person when she wasn't being controlled by demons. I had asked pastors, missionaries, ministry directors, Christian and non-Christian counselors, and anyone else who would listen for answers. But we still kept coming to a dead end.

I began to regularly lie facedown on the floor of my bedroom in prayer, begging the Lord to provide some direction. I wasn't a quitter, but something had to give.

After praying one day I remembered Roxanne telling me that she kept stuff at her mom's house back in Louisiana. I wasn't sure if any of it related to her life in a coven, but it was worth pursuing. Maybe one of these items was what was leaving the door open for the demons to come back inside her or not leave her at all.

I asked Roxanne what she had left there, but she was hesitant to answer at first. I was a desperate man, and when she saw how serious I was she told me. There was a robe that she wore when performing ceremonies, some jewelry, and *The Book of Shadows*.

There are many forms and branches of witchcraft. *The Book of Shadows* is not normally associated with satanic groups but is the handbook for the more contemporary New Age and Wicca movements. It was created by Gerald Gardner in the late 1940s or early 1950s and is filled with rites and spells and tips on magic, though not the kind of violent ritualistic behavior described by Roxanne as happening in her coven. I note this to make sure I don't paint everyone who claims to be a witch or part of Wicca as a satanist. This book is not the place to define and distinguish true religion, false religion, satanic religion, made-up religion, or anything else. You know my perspective as a Christian. So, I don't apologize in stating my belief that *The Book of Shadows* is clearly not of God, has many rites and rituals I find morally offensive and even dangerous, and, I firmly believe, served as a doorway for Satan to remain in Roxanne's life.

I told Roxanne we needed to go and get that stuff and destroy it. The three of us could start early on Saturday and make the long drive to her mom's house, destroy everything, and head home the same day. It would be a long day, but if this was what was keeping Roxanne from finding her freedom—and I thought it was—it would be well worth the effort.

The next day at work I told a couple of coworkers

about the plan to drive to Louisiana to destroy all the satanic items Roxanne had at her mom's house. Everyone agreed it was a good idea. It might not work, but I didn't know what else to do at this point.

I went to the main studio to prepare for my midday shift. I saw my request line blinking. In a radio studio the phones blink because you cannot have the phone ringing on the air when you are doing your broadcast. It develops great peripheral vision in most disc jockeys. I picked up the phone and said a preoccupied "Hello," still multitasking.

There was nothing on the phone for at least a couple of seconds. I was about to hang up when I heard that dreadful voice of a demon.

"You'll never make it to Louisiana."

How did this thing know of our plans?

"You'll never make it," the demon continued. "I'll kill you before you get to her mom's house. I'll move her *Book of Shadows* so you cannot destroy it."

That was all he had to say before he hung up. But this demon continued to call a number of times each day leading up to the road trip. The message was the same each time: You won't make it to Roxanne's mom's house alive. If you do, everything you are looking for will be moved.

After the demon called one day and had once again hung up on me, I looked at a coworker and jokingly said, "He thinks he is so bad and bold; I think I'll command him to bring me the jewelry in Jesus' name so I don't have to make the drive."

That was the only time I can think of that I was being flip and not taking this seriously. The phone rang just as soon as I said that. It was the demon again and he said: "Your request is my command."

The phone went dead. My colleague and I just looked at each other in amazement. Immediately I asked the Lord's forgiveness for joking about something so intense and serious.

I arrived home from work that night and went inside through the garage. As I walked toward the door leading into the mudroom beside the kitchen, I noticed a few metallic things in the middle of the floor. I knelt down and saw pieces of jewelry in the shapes of pentagrams, moons, stars, and other shapes and symbols I didn't recognize and couldn't describe. It crossed my mind that the demon had actually brought Roxanne's jewelry to my house, far faster than any overnight delivery service. But that would have been impossible.

I called my wife and Roxanne to come into the garage to take a look. I pointed to the items, still lying on the floor. I asked if anyone knew how they got here.

"How did you get my jewelry?" Roxanne asked with a shocked expression on her face.

When I told her what had happened at the radio station, even she was surprised and afraid.

We took the jewelry out into the driveway with a hammer. I told Roxanne I thought we needed to destroy the stuff. I expected an argument or some other form of resistance, but she immediately agreed, nodding her head up and down.

We scooped up all the jewelry in a shovel so we didn't have to touch it and headed for the driveway. Roxanne picked up the hammer to destroy the stuff herself.

"If I want to be free, I have to do it myself," she said.

I was incredibly proud of her. This was just one of many moments that seemed to make the pain of our battles worthwhile. She had a look of determination. I used the edge of the shovel to scrape the jewelry into a tidy pile. Concentrating hard, she lifted the hammer to strike the first blow. Things never went easy when it came to Roxanne and demons, and this was no exception. Her arm froze at the highest point where she would bring the hammer down with all her strength. A voice was screaming urgently from inside her: "No, no, no, no, no! Don't do it."

Her arm was shaking. An invisible force seemed to be restraining her. Then she struck a blow.

Voices cried and screamed and cursed. But Roxanne continued to hammer away. Maybe this was a therapeutic moment for her, to literally smash symbols of years of brokenness and captivity.

It took a long time to make sure each piece of jewelry was smashed beyond recognition. This was a difficult process for her and me, but mostly for her. Each ring, necklace, bracelet, charm (or amulet), and items I didn't recognize had a hold on Roxanne, and a demon appeared to be attached to each and every one. Some screeched in anger, others in agony, others in pitiful sobs for mercy, and some in all of the above.

It was a real battle out in our driveway that evening. My biggest hope was that this would finally give Roxanne freedom from the demons. I wanted to see every one of them leave her life forever. Surely they had to realize that despite the threats and battles at every turn, we were not giving up.

The next morning I went to work and told my coworkers what had happened. A few looked skeptical when I told them the demon brought the jewelry to us in little more than the time it took me to drive home.

I was on air for my shift only two or three minutes when the request line began to flash. I didn't want to answer, but it was my show so I had to.

"Hi, you've reached Bill Scott," I said in my chirpy radio voice.

"Did you receive my gift last night?"

My heart skipped a beat.

"I can bring more tonight if that is what you want," he continued. "I can bring all the jewelry to you, my friend."

One, I was not his friend; and two, I didn't want jewelry delivered to my home a few pieces at a time.

"I bind you in Jesus' name," I said with all the force I could muster. "You will bring no more items to my home."

The line went dead. I didn't want the jewelry delivered to my home, even if it would save us a long road trip. But I also knew my wife and I wouldn't be home all the time, and I just didn't think it was a good idea for Roxanne to get her hands on items from her past with no one there to support the commitment she had made to destroy anything that would give Satan access to her life.

Any hesitation about making the trip to Louisiana that very weekend was gone. I was now totally convinced that these items had to be the open door we needed to slam shut. Why else the cursing and begging from the demons?

I wasn't looking forward to the twenty-hour round-trip drive, but at this point I would do anything to make this stop. I wanted a normal life back for my wife and me, but mostly this was for Roxanne's sake.

We left at four in the morning Saturday to make the trip to Louisiana. I had no idea what in the world was going to happen. Would we make it safely? The demons promised to block our path. Would we find *The Book of Shadows* and the rest of the jewelry? Demons promised to move it. Would Roxanne be up for the battle? She had done well so far, but she still wasn't free of evil spirits. I had no idea what to expect, but we knew we had to do it.

We arrived safely. After meeting her mother—who was very happy and surprised to see Roxanne—we walked into the back of the house to Roxanne's room. We found everything she said would be there. The demons had lied. They had claimed power and control that they did not have.

We brought everything outside to a patio in the back and began to destroy items one by one. Like the work we did in the driveway in front of my house, it was a long and arduous process. Some things were harder than others for Roxanne to destroy. *The Book of Shadows* was the hardest. Much as was the case when it was time to renounce Lacey, I think there was a part of Roxanne that didn't want to let go of something that had been such a big part of her life, even if it had been a destructive influence.

We kept Roxanne surrounded in prayer the whole time. Even her mother prayed with us. I couldn't help but wonder why she had kept all these things for Roxanne. Had she not experienced the demon activity, too? Surprisingly there was a Bible, some Christian music cassettes, and other Christian items in Roxanne's room. How could such a clash of worldviews be present in the same place—and the same person?

I didn't have time to think about it. We were there to destroy anything that might be giving evil spirits access to

Roxanne's life. It's hard to convey the weariness of that endeavor.

We looked around. I believed everything satanic had been destroyed. Hopefully this was the final thing that needed to happen for Roxanne to be free. We held hands in a circle and prayed for Roxanne, for her mom, for Satan to be bound, and for safe travel on the ten-hour drive ahead.

CHAPTER 18

The Answer Is Revealed

We had accomplished what we'd set out to do. We destroyed items that had been a part of Roxanne's life in a satanic coven. We were home safely. Roxanne had a job and her own car. We had located an apartment for her to live in, and she would be moving out in just a few days. It would again be just my wife and me in our home. It was finally time for things to truly go back to normal.

But not for Roxanne. The demons were still present in her life. How could this be? *Someone, please help this woman*, was all I could think and pray. I'm not a quitter. But I was tired. It had been eighteen months since we met Roxanne. You can battle for only so long before you are totally exhausted. Roxanne was not in my home anymore. How much more did God want me to do to help her? Did I have any more responsibility for what happened to her?

I thought back to the people recorded in Roxanne's notebook: preachers and youth pastors, ministry directors, staff members and volunteers, Christian couples and individuals committed to helping others. I talked to many of them. The patterns found in those conversations were of divorce, illness, churches splitting, ministries folding, ministers falling to temptation. There was a path of destruction in Roxanne's wake. She was both victim and active participant. She took orders from Abaddon the destroyer, Satan's general.

Even my own church had begun having major problems with conflict among pastor and staff and congregation over the direction the church was heading. Friends took opposing sides and became enemies. It became such a mess that eventually our church split.

I am definitely not attributing blame to Roxanne the real person. But Roxanne the one who was inhabited by demons? To this day, I believe she was a pawn in a battle to create strife and conflict. If, as we noted earlier, the world will know that we are disciples because of our love for one another, what will the world believe when it appears we hate one another?

Our radio station had been like a family to me, but the director resigned under pressure and my job was in jeopardy. I put out my résumé and landed a similar job ninety miles away. Six days a week I made the 180-mile round-trip.

It was becoming clear that many important things in our lives were beginning to fall apart. The church had split. Our friends were scattering to other churches. I had just begun a new job with a long commute. And then there was Roxanne. We were still trying to help her, still holding on to the hope she could be free.

Once Roxanne got her own apartment, she had a lot of free time that was not accounted for as it was when she lived in the group home or with us. I found out that she was calling a national ministry hotline for help. I wanted to compare notes on where we thought Roxanne was on her journey, so I called the hotline asking if they had heard of Roxanne. They were just like the people from Roxanne's notebook I had called. Cautious and wary, they wanted to know who I was and what I wanted. They, too, had experienced the voices and wrath of demons and threats from self-identified witches and warlocks.

I explained who I was and where I worked and why I was calling. I got a return call from Randy, the one who talked to Roxanne most often. He had heard from Roxanne just about every day for the last week. From what he described, it sounded like they were dealing with the same Roxanne I had first met eighteen months earlier. At one point he and a group had been on the phone with her for twenty-four hours straight, battling demons and trying to help her.

I had to consider the possibility that we had not helped Roxanne at all. We were just one more stop in a repeating cycle. Our church, with a huge local, regional, and national reputation, was splitting. If this was truly Roxanne's original goal, since she had succeeded, would she now be moving on to the next victim?

I still didn't feel we could give up on her. I think it was because I was afraid of defeat. And I truly felt that it was my duty as a Christian not to give up on Roxanne.

I know part of the reason I didn't want to give up was that Roxanne would often show just enough improvement to convince me victory was possible. Roxanne continued to live on her own, struggling with demons on a regular basis. She would go to church with us on most Sundays, and as she worshipped with raised hands, you could still hear demons growling if you sat near enough to her.

Someone at the new radio station knew a little bit of what I was going through and said, "You should listen to this national nightly Christian radio talk show. The host has this one girl he has been talking to almost every night for four weeks now. She says she is part of a coven that practices satanic witchcraft."

That was the last thing I wanted to listen to. I'd experienced it firsthand for the last year and a half. I gave it no thought.

Over the next few weeks several more people told me about this radio guy who kept getting calls from a girl who lived in a coven. I still ignored the suggestion that I should listen to the program.

Finally one of the new guys I worked with came into my studio and said, "I think you need to listen to this radio station. The girl who keeps calling in sounds exactly like the woman you are working with."

That got my attention. I could no longer ignore what people had been trying to tell me. I asked myself if this could be Roxanne calling from her apartment. I think I already knew the answer in my heart.

So I listened to this program. Two minutes into the show I could hear Roxanne. She had the host turning somersaults to help her. Who wouldn't? She was to become a human sacrifice on Halloween.

As I sat in my recliner and listened that night, I realized why so many people were buzzing about this radio show. Roxanne told her story incredibly well, and I'm sure she had the listening audience on the edge of their seats. It made me really mad.

I called the radio's toll-free number. I told the person who was answering the phone I knew who the girl was and wanted to help. They ignored me and hung up. I'm sure they received a lot of prank phone calls while Roxanne was on the air.

It took several more attempts, but I finally got through to the producer of the program. She came to the phone, and I told her there were some things she needed to know about Roxanne. She was very quiet. She told me later she was scared I might be part of Roxanne's coven and was trying to keep them away from her. I told the producer what Christian station I worked at and gave a few pastors' names as references. I told her to check my information and call me back.

She called back later and asked me, "How do you know Roxanne?"

I gave her a brief history of what had happened with us and how we were still trying to help her.

"Roxanne is not going to be sacrificed. She is calling you from her home. I absolutely believe the demons in her life are real, but the story she is telling you is not true."

At first the producer didn't believe me. In the back of her mind she probably realized that if Roxanne's story was proved to be a fabrication, it would be an embarrassment to their radio ministry.

"We can call Roxanne right now if you want to," I said.

"You have her number?" I heard a gasp as she asked that.

"Of course I have her number. She goes to church with us every Sunday, and we see her a couple more times during the week. I also know where she lives, since my wife and I helped her get set up in her apartment. I am telling you I know who Roxanne is. She isn't a young teen. She isn't going to be sacrificed. She is probably at home watching TV right now."

She decided to place the call to Roxanne. She conferenced me in. Roxanne answered the phone and was shocked when the producer of the program identified herself. Roxanne tried to keep the charade of being trapped in a coven going, but the producer broke in and said, "I have a friend who wants to talk with you. Here's Bill."

Roxanne was quiet. She knew that she had been caught. She confessed that she made up everything about the coven but said she had no control over what she did and wasn't sure why she did it. I could tell the program director didn't know what to say or do. If you work in the media, Christian or mainstream, you will have to conduct damage control sooner or later. Roxanne had been one of their main callers and had boosted their listenership tremendously. She had listeners mesmerized. To tell them it was a hoax wasn't going to go over well at all.

Roxanne had fooled smarter people than me, yet in my experiences with her, there was likewise no way to say the demons weren't real. There was no way to fake or stage things I saw and heard and even felt. Roxanne wasn't there when a spirit bumped my leg in the night.

I remained convinced she was a pawn in Satan's strategy to destroy Christian churches, ministries, and couples. What I didn't know was whether or not Roxanne was doing this on purpose. Did she know she was being used this way? Was she aware of all that was going on? I really didn't know, but I was still determined to figure that out.

I called a few of my friends who had been through this entire experience with me and asked if we could meet to pray on a daily basis with one single request, that God would bring someone to us who would shed light on what was going on and what we were to do next.

It was a Friday. I was driving the ninety-mile trail for my Friday shift. I had decided I would spend the night because I had to be back to work the next morning early for a remote. A local pastor and his wife said I could stay with them. They were good friends, so I figured this would be a fun night. Work finished, I headed over to my friends' home. I had never shared Roxanne's story with them and didn't plan on doing so that night.

My pastor friend and I sat down in the living room after dinner and chatted about sports, politics, and weather. But somehow the conversation made it to the subject of Roxanne. Before I knew what was happening, I'd told him the whole story. The words just poured out. He was my therapist that night.

When I finished—a couple of hours later—he just stared at me. Had I bored him to death? Did he think I was crazy?

"Bill, I know what is happening, and I know the answer you are looking for. You are looking for an answer, aren't you?"

I just nodded. I was speechless. Could this be true? After all this time, was there really someone who could help me? Had my prayers been answered through this friend? Anxiously I waited for what he would say next.

"Bill, Satan is not after Roxanne, he already has her. He is after you. Satan wants you because you are the one who is called to ministry."

This was not what I expected to hear. I was looking for a profound answer that would tell me how to save Roxanne.

"But I believe Roxanne can be saved," I said.

"Good," he answered. "I hope you're right. But it's time for you to back off."

"I'm not a quitter."

"Neither is God," he said. "But He doesn't force people to receive His gift of grace against their will. Bill, Roxanne doesn't want help right now. Words are great, but just look at her actions. She is still here to destroy."

I had gathered friends to pray that God would lead us to a person who could provide me with the answers I needed to do what was best for Roxanne. Now that he was sitting in front of me, I wasn't sure I wanted to hear the answer.

"You don't know what I've invested in Roxanne," I said.

"But maybe you don't understand what Roxanne has invested in you," he said, with an emphasis on *you*.

"Bill, you've told me yourself several times that Roxanne is there to destroy ministers and ministries."

"It's not her, it's the demons," I said.

"The demons are real and powerful," he answered. "But she still has a choice in this. You may be right. She may be very close to wanting to be free. But it's obvious that right now she's not there. She will never be free from evil spirits until she wants to be."

I wanted to argue with him some more. But what he was saying made too much sense. I found myself believing him. And when I did, it felt like a million pounds had been lifted from me. I was not a failure. I was not responsible. Roxanne knew she was being used by Satan. She was sent to destroy me and keep me from helping hurting people through the ministry God had called me to. That didn't make me particularly special. I wasn't the only one she had sought to destroy. In fact, I felt like I was at the back of a long line of people she had sought to sabotage, including my wife. It was late. I called my wife and said, "I have the answer. I know what is going on." We talked for a while, and she also felt that a huge burden had been lifted off her.

It was late Saturday afternoon by the time I returned home. I was excited to talk with my wife about the things I had learned while at our friend's house. We called a few of the people who had been praying to share with them what we had learned. Everyone seemed to think this was the answer we'd been looking for.

So what was the next step? We needed to call Roxanne and have her come over to the house so we could confront her. I still had a heart to reach her. I wanted to see her be free from evil spirits. I wasn't angry on any level. Yes, she was sent to destroy us, but I could forgive her for that. I just wanted to see her move forward in life.

CHAPTER 19

It's Over

I was very apprehensive at the thought of confronting Roxanne. What would she say? What would she do? Would there suddenly be a new outburst of demonic raging, cursing, and blasphemy? I had worked hard to keep any satanic activity outside my home. Would she admit to attempting to destroy my family and the ministry?

Even though I knew this relationship had to end now, and I was doing the right thing, I felt like a failure. Even if she was a willing pawn, I didn't believe Roxanne really knew what Satan was doing through her. I knew that deep down inside she was a beautiful person. I wasn't fighting Roxanne; I was fighting the demons that were sent to destroy her and everything in her path.

I didn't have a long time to be nervous. Before I could make a phone call to Roxanne to ask her to come over, I heard a car pull up in my driveway. I looked outside and saw Roxanne step out of her car. She started walking up to our front door. I could tell by the look on her face that she wasn't very happy. There was a knock on the door and I let her in. She just looked at me and said, "It's over. I am leaving now." I asked her where she was heading. She just said, "east."

As we walked outside and down the sidewalk, I could

see that her car was packed. I told her that we were not angry, we loved her, and we wanted only God's best for her. She wouldn't look at me. She had already checked out mentally, and I'm not sure she heard a word I said. She just repeated that her time was up here and she was leaving. The demons that controlled her life knew we had figured out what they had been doing through her all along.

East. I prayed for every church, ministry, pastor, and married couple east of me.

I wish this was the part of the story where I could tell you we won the battle for Roxanne. The last eighteen months had been life-changing, challenging, and emotionally devastating at times. At that moment in time, all our efforts and prayers seemed to have been for naught. We hadn't saved Roxanne.

I'll never forget watching Roxanne slide into her car, put it in gear, and pull out of our driveway. I watched her drive off until the car disappeared around a corner. It was a bittersweet moment. I was glad that it was over, but I didn't feel any sense of victory because I knew Roxanne still needed help.

CHAPTER 20

I Still Have Questions

Writing this book has been my first attempt in twenty-one years to describe in detail my eighteen-month experience with Roxanne. It's brought back a flood of memories—mostly bad, and emotions—mostly sad. I have shared this story in bits and pieces with a few friends over the years, but other than my pastor friend who told me I had to let Roxanne go, never from start to finish. I lived the events but still have questions today. Most have to do with Roxanne.

How did Roxanne get involved in satanism? Did she ever live in a coven? If not, was she abused? And who were the people who seemed to support her and provide backup? If they weren't a coven, what kind of organization did they have? Did some part of Roxanne have a sincere desire to follow Jesus Christ? If some parts of Roxanne's story were a hoax, did that make everything a hoax? Where did she go after she drove off that day? Did she continue a pattern where her presence encouraged the splitting of churches, the moral failure of ministers, and the breakup of marriages?

I've also had some very personal questions about my perceptions and role in all of this. Why was I singled out to be the front person to work with Roxanne? What could I have done differently? Well, I'm not quite as headstrong and stubborn now as I was then, so maybe I would have had less ego involved and been wiser as to when it was time to back away.

My most significant personal question is really not very deep. I've simply wondered why there has never been any further occurrence of spiritual warfare—as waged against overt demons—in my life.

How often does Satan really work through overt demonic activity? Are there seasons? There were numerous reports of satanic covens and occult activity during the time this event occurred in my life. Has Satan changed strategies? Are there more effective ways for him to undermine faith and take as many to hell with him as he can? And what about reports of satanic activity? How accurate are they? I know what happened to me and I know evil spirits were at work, but I wasn't right on everything. For example, I don't think now that there was ever a coven with breeders and human sacrifice. Maybe somewhere. But not near where I lived.

Because of the amount of time we spent with Roxanne, I have continued to wonder about the relationship between demon possession and mental illness. I don't think a multiple personality disorder could generate the voices of a chorus of demons or authentic wild animal sounds in a single person. I also don't think that would give a woman Roxanne's size the strength to lift a 220-pound man off his feet and hold him with one hand.

There has always been a fascination with demon possession and exorcism—from books to films to music to true-life accounts like mine. Hollywood has its own take on demon possession. For example *The Rite* recently came out, starring Anthony Hopkins, and was a top-grossing film nationwide at the box office during the first weekend of its release.

I don't claim to be an expert on the work of Satan to-day—though I do suspect his strategies change from time to time—nor do I have the desire to be one. But in addition to my questions, I have learned a few things through meeting Roxanne, an extended encounter that I think of as a singular event in my life. Let me summarize a few of the points of view others have about satanic phenomena with a few comments of my own.

A study of adult beliefs conducted by the Barna Group reported:

> Four out of ten Christians (40%) strongly agreed that Satan "is not a living being but is a symbol of evil." An additional two out of ten Christians (19%) said they "agree somewhat" with that perspective. A minority of Christians indicated that they believe Satan is real by disagreeing with the statement: one-quarter (25%) disagreed strongly and about one-tenth (9%) disagreed somewhat. The remaining 7% were not sure what they believe about the existence of Satan.[1]

So it's not surprising that the majority of people are fundamentally skeptical about most if not all reports of satanic activity. Even if they believe in Satan, they still might agree that reports and personal testimonies of experiences with evil spirits are a product of a fevered imagination. I wouldn't have said so at the time, but maybe this described me before meeting Roxanne.

Skeptics would explain their position by saying that since the beginning of recorded history some kind of prince of darkness has been found in myths and stories. And in most myths, calamity—from bad crops to an injured foot—has been explained through Satan's intervention or that of his spiritual warriors. Because people always have been and always will be interested in dark mysterious forces, stories will continue to be told and to evolve.

For example, authors and filmmakers know that people are drawn to conflict. The categories of conflict are: man vs. man; man vs. himself; man vs. nature; and man vs. God. Well, what greater conflict can there be than for "man" to fight the forces of evil? These creative types are prime examples of people who create terrifying images of evil, knowing full well they are fiction.

I would argue that the fact that almost every culture in the history of humankind has recognized some teaching on Satan suggests we ought to believe in him.

And what about credible people who report firsthand encounters with evil spirits? How do the skeptics explain these stories? The skeptic might simply state that some individuals have been "brainwashed" since childhood to believe in Satan and demons. When bad things happen to them, the person naturally attributes it to the work of evil spirits. The skeptics might agree these individuals are sincere, but would argue they are misguided and their perceptions of what happened are wrong.

Some skeptics claim that reports of satanic activity are fundamentally an invention of religious folks who want to scare people in order to control them—or to cash in from the notoriety of fighting evil. The skeptics agree with Anton LaVey's *Book of Satan* that says belief in Satan is good "business" for Christians.

I can't quantify it, but I think most skeptics simply think the person reporting satanic activity is misguided and a logical explanation hasn't been found.

I would like to note there's one very compelling reason many people are so skeptical of tales of satanic activity— lack of evidence. This just heightens the claims that reports of evil spirits are outrageous and exaggerated.

For example, if cults were sacrificing children at the levels some Christians have claimed, there would be a huge number of kids missing, many more than are currently reported. And where are all the bodies being disposed?

Dr. Gail S. Goodman, of the University of California, Davis, conducted a study for the National Center on Child Abuse and Neglect titled *Characteristics and Sources of Allegations of Ritualistic Child Abuse*, which surveyed more than twelve thousand psychologists, law enforcement officers, and social workers, and failed to find a single credible or confirmed allegation of abuse by organized satanic cults.[2] I personally feel this report is skewed to disprove the notion that any ritual abuse occurs and that the proof they are demanding would not have shown up in their questions and methodology.

But I can't argue that outlandish claims have encouraged an overall skepticism. It's this skepticism that has explained in part my reluctance to share this story for more than twenty years.

Others believe that satanism is a form of mental illness and that what is often described as demon possession is actually multiple personality disorder (MPD) or, as it is more often called today, dissociative identity disorder (DID).

An MPD diagnosis means at least one "alter" personality exists that can control the thoughts, feelings, and behavior of the individual, completely separate from and in the place of the person's primary identity. Many times the person doesn't remember anything he or she has done while the "alter" personality has taken over, finding themselves in places and situations that shock them as much as those who know them.

MPD is usually thought to be a coping mechanism, often in response to repressed memories of childhood abuse. The pain is so intense the individual forms boundaries by creating new selves or identities. When confronted with or reminded of the extreme hurt, the thinking is that the individual "leaves" to get away from it and lets another self handle things for a while. This is a gross oversimplification, and clearly there is much more to this extremely complex disorder. How many personalities can function within a single person? Some clinical reports have noted thousands of identities in one person.

There are doctors and psychiatrists who debunk MPD, but I don't have a hard time believing in the disorder, especially in those who have endured unbelievable abuse. I am quite certain, however, that MPD cannot turn lights on and off throughout a house or do many of the other things I witnessed and experienced.

I am equally certain that it was demons we were dealing with when it came to Roxanne. But I also believe we could have been witnessing a combination of MPD and demons pulling her life and world in so many different directions.

In stark contrast to the skeptics are the people who believe evil spirits are responsible for almost everything that happens in the material world.

As I've said, I'm not a theologian, so I'll simply reiterate that I don't think overt satanic activity in the form of demon possession is a common way for Satan to work in the world today. At least not in our culture. He has too many other ways to take humans down the path of ruin.

Gary Thomas, who was trained by the Vatican to be an exorcist, pastors in the Silicon Valley of California. His experiences were the inspiration behind the 2011 blockbuster movie starring Anthony Hopkins called *The Rite*. In a *USA Today* article by Maria Puente, Thomas was quoted as saying he had conducted exorcisms on five people since he was trained five years ago. Also quoted in the article was Bishop Thomas Paprocki, who stated that "only a small fraction of requests for an exorcism should be granted because only a small fraction of cases—maybe less than 5%—actually involve demonic possession."[3] Bottom line, I have no idea how large the presence of satanic activity is in this day and age. But I do believe it and covens, rituals, sacrifices, spells, amulets, magic, and other forms of witchcraft, satanic or otherwise, exist and are practiced at every level of society, including poor people, rich people, teachers, government workers, politicians, and housewives.

What is the appeal?

If Christianity calls for us to submit to the will of God as expressed in Jesus' prayer on the cross—"not as I will, but as You will" (Matt. 26:39)—then satanism teaches that there are incantations, spells, and rites that force the spirit world to submit to us and help us get what we want. At least that's the appeal, even if it doesn't turn out to be the reality.

Some reports of satanic activity are made up. Some reports of satanic activity are probably mental illness. But some reports of satanic activity are very real—and can include mental illness. I definitely do not believe that all accounts of satanic activity are fabricated, or I would have turned in this book as fiction.

There is a real spiritual world, including evil spirits, out there, and, as I experienced, sometimes you cannot choose to ignore it.

CHAPTER 21

Another Call

This book began with the story of a phone call, and now it ends with a story of a phone call. You see, in order to publish this book, I needed to find Roxanne again. I needed to ask her to sign a release giving me permission to tell this story.

I didn't think it would be a big deal to locate her, but after several weeks of looking through every person locator I could find both online and off, there was no sign of her.

I hired a private investigator. Certainly this professional could find her because she had access to databases we didn't even know existed. Two weeks went by and nothing. In fact, she told me that she couldn't figure out how Roxanne could have disappeared so completely. She wondered if she had died, but a search of death records was just as futile.

I finally told my wife I really didn't think we were going to find her. Janet's response was, "Here is a list of churches in the area we know she last lived. Let's divide it and start calling."

Amazingly, the first church Janet called was it! Roxanne actually attended their church, and they said they would be more than happy to let her know I was looking for her. Reality then set in; was I really ready for this?

The path of destruction that lay in the wake of having dealt with all those demons was tragic. Of the seven primary couples involved in trying to help Roxanne over those eighteen months, six of the marriages ended in divorce, including mine. The church we attended split and has never again had the impact it once had in its community and on America and the world.

I am not stating that our involvement with Roxanne was the primary, direct cause of all these divorces. But I did call a number of people from her notebook and learned that many of them suffered the same result. So I don't disregard that working with Roxanne played a role.

Now it was twenty-one years later. I pressed the Answer button and heard a familiar voice. Roxanne was on the line. We had talked only one time on the phone for a minute or so since she'd driven out of my driveway and my life. But now we were on the phone together again. We both felt somewhat awkward at first.

I was scared that this phone call would be much like the first call twenty-one years ago. I expected to hear demons tell me I would never write the book or share Roxanne's story, and that they would hurt my family. My heart pounded as the conversation began. Was I opening Pandora's box once again? I didn't want to hear those inhuman voices. I didn't want to experience evil, the coldness of evil, the heaviness of evil again in my life. It seemed like a lifetime waiting for the conversation to begin. After a few seconds of small talk, Roxanne opened up to tell me where she was in life. She had been involved in a great church in her area for nearly five years. She went to Christian counseling and therapy every week. She shared that her mental state was up and down, but the demons were gone. Completely. She had not invited them back, and in Jesus' name they had no access to her heart and mind.

I can't describe the joy I felt. Roxanne let me know several times she was still a mess, but she said it with a grace and humor I had never heard from her before. It was so obvious she was now on a path of freedom and healing. Her journey had taken a miraculous turn.

I had always known that deep down Roxanne was a wonderful person who had experienced unimaginable abuses in her life, thus giving Satan a foothold that turned into a stronghold. Now here I was, talking to that person I always knew was there. Roxanne knows that because of the road she's traveled, her life may never look and feel completely "normal"—and a lot of us can relate to that. But she has a quiet confidence that she is free and on the road to growing in Christ. Roxanne made a choice, the same choice we are all faced with, to walk with God. In Joshua 24:15 we hear the words of God's servant to God's people: "Choose for yourselves this day whom you will serve...But as for me and my house, we will serve the LORD."

Roxanne had chosen.

We continued to talk. I explained to her my reason for wanting to locate her. She graciously consented to sign the document that would allow me to tell this story.

Though my part in the battle for Roxanne ended twenty-one years earlier, as I pushed the End Call button, I reflected that all along, my real battle was for my own soul and ministry.

There is a battle that goes on every day for each of us. It probably doesn't feel as dramatic as being confronted by a satanic witch. But it's real nonetheless. Every one of us is in the middle of some form of spiritual warfare right now. Satan doesn't always come as a "roaring lion" (1 Pet. 5:8); rather, he often shows up as an "angel of light" (2 Cor. 11:14).

We began this book with Ephesians 6:12:

> We do not wrestle against flesh and blood, but against principalities, against powers, against the rulers of the darkness of this world, against spiritual hosts of wickedness in the heavenly places.

Just because you haven't seen demons or haven't encountered someone who has been in the occult doesn't mean the battle for you and your family isn't real. In my call-in show and travels I have found there is a hidden world out there that very few people talk about. Scripture is very clear that Satan is battling against the church, families, marriages, our kids, and ministries. In many cases he appears to be winning.

There have been times when we might be very aware of satanic activity because it is overt and aggressive—but I am certain there are more times when we are barely aware it is occurring. Satan's work just might be easier and more effective when we are lulled into thinking he isn't even there.

Roxanne was possessed by demons. She invited them inside her to be her spirit guides and to control her life. Most of us haven't done anything so dramatic and dangerous. But I believe it is still possible for spiritual evil to control any area of our lives that we are willing to hand over to dark forces.

I have talked with people over the years on my national radio program who are addicted to porn, drugs, and alcohol. Others are cheating on their spouses. Some are stealing from their companies. I've not sensed that any of them are demon-possessed. But again, the final battle is for our souls, whatever form it may take.

Some reading this book may be controlled by Satan right now. The bottom line is that if every area of your life doesn't belong to God, it is vulnerable to the work of Satan. The good news is there is freedom for anyone wanting to break addictions or anything else that is not right in his or her life. Roxanne handed herself over to so many evil things—but she isn't alone. Alongside Roxanne, we have a decision to make: Whom will we serve? She eventually made the decision to let the love of God make her a new person through Christ Jesus.

Some tell me they don't believe there is spiritual warfare going on today. From the very opening of this book, I have pointed out that I wasn't raised to believe in demons. I wasn't disposed to interpret events around me as satanic activity. You can believe what you wish about spiritual warfare, but I would encourage you to simply look around at the obvious. Broken marriages and families, addictions, a prevailing spirit of anger...I think it's hard *not* to believe we are under attack.

You don't have to remain in bondage to addictions of the flesh or emotions. You can take control of your life by the power of Christ. Today you can begin your journey of healing and freedom.

Ten Spiritual and Life Lessons

The eighteen-month journey I took with Roxanne was the most intense and challenging time of my life. I never would have thought it possible that I would be thrust into the realm of demonic activity like I was. I had no clue these kinds of things happened and that Satan could exert so much power. But if it hadn't been for my experiences with Roxanne, I would never have had the opportunity to see God's awesome power so dramatically. Again and again He rescued me spiritually and even physically.

And He taught me some incredible spiritual and life lessons.

1. Pray for Salvation

God has made a way for you to experience His love forever. Why is it important to have Jesus as Lord? When it comes to satanic activity, the Bible says if you cast a demon out, after a while it will come back to you looking for a home, and if that home is empty, it will return with seven more spirits worse than itself. By accepting Jesus as Lord, the home is filled. All of us need Jesus, not just for our salvation but for our daily lives. Jesus paid the price for our wrongdoing so we can spend eternity in heaven with him.

2. Trust in the Power of God for Deliverance in Life

Satan is strong, but God is stronger: "You are of God, little children, and have overcome them, because He who is in you is greater than he who is in the world" (1 John 4:4).

The Bible is very clear that anyone can be set free from an evil spirit. God's power is something that Satan cannot match on any level. But a person has to want to be set free and accept God into his or her life.

3. Protect Your Home

I was naive. I should never have taken a witch into my home. Your home is not the place to deal with someone who is involved in satanic activity. Guard your home from all evil influences, including that which can be accessed through radio, television, and the Internet.

4. Don't Assume Problematic or Even Bizarre Behavior Is a Result of Satanic Activity

I've heard horror stories of well-intentioned Christians trying to cast demons from a spouse or child who is experiencing depression or some other mental illness. To assume that demons are involved in all behavioral problems can be very destructive, and may also undermine someone else's confidence in you and their faith in God, as well as do incredible psychological and spiritual damage. My experience was that demons won't make you guess if what you are seeing is demonic activity or not. If you do feel there is a person close to you who is demon-possessed, be sure to gather a group of mature and spiritual Christians to discuss and pray about the situation before you consider any form of intervention.

5. Recognize That Satanic Activity Is Real

I know there are a lot of people who have sensed evil when they have heard things or felt strange and assumed they were crazy or could never tell anyone what they were experiencing. I want you to know you are not alone. We all need to be reminded that we live in a spiritual world. Just because we don't see Satan on a daily basis does not mean he is not alive and working against us. We are surrounded by the spirit world. Angels and demons are among us. We are to live not in fear, but rather in a state of daily dependence on God to meet our every need, including spiritual needs.

6. Fight Boldly with the Armor of God

I have been asked, "If you met someone like Roxanne today, would you go through it all again?" My answer is simple: Yes, but only if I was sure God had called me to intervene in the person's life. I would never go looking for a demon-possessed person, nor would I bring them into my home. Fight boldly, but never forget to fight with God's power. Ephesians 6:11 reminds us to fight with the full armor of God: "Put on the full armor of God so that you can take your stand against the devil's schemes" (NIV).

7. Break Any and All Agreements with Satan

You don't have to be in witchcraft or the occult to give Satan strongholds in your life. Are there areas of your life you have no control over? Have you told yourself that you will never be free from certain thoughts and habits? If you answer yes, those are agreements you have made with Satan that need to be broken. There is power in believing what is true—and unfortunately there is a different kind of power in not believing the truth. In Jesus' name, break those unhealthy agreements and replace them with affirmations of what God declares to be true: "Then you will experience for yourselves the truth, and the truth will free you" (John 8:32 The Message).

8. Deal with the Pain of Your Past

The past isn't the past if you are still letting it control your life today. Many say time heals all wounds. That is simply not a true statement. Time heals nothing if you are not on a road to healing. Many are dealing with emotional wounds and loss from the past. It's important to give the past to God and ask Him to heal you. Find a trusted Christian friend or counselor to walk you through the healing process. Hurt will always distort your decisions and views of the future if not dealt with. This will continue to give Satan a hold and an open door through which to cause problems in your life.

Until you understand who you are in Christ, you can never find true freedom. If you are a believer, you are indeed a new creation. Now you need to learn to walk as that new creation in order to begin your journey. Freedom is for everyone, including you.

9. Know the Word

The importance of being in God's Word on a regular basis cannot be overemphasized. Satan is counting on the fact that you don't truly know God's Word. It's easy to buy the lie when you don't know the truth. The psalmist expresses the importance of knowing God's Word beautifully:

> How can a young person stay on the path of purity?
> By living according to your word.
> I seek you with all my heart;
> do not let me stray from your commands.
> I have hidden your word in my heart
> that I might not sin against you.
> Praise be to you, O LORD;
> teach me your decrees.

With my lips I recount
all the laws that come from your mouth.
I rejoice in following your statutes
as one rejoices in great riches.
I meditate on your precepts
and consider your ways.
I delight in your decrees;
I will not neglect your word. (Psalm 119:9–16
NIV)

10. Find a Local Church

Get involved in a Christian fellowship. Being part of a good church is vital for your growth. We all need someone with whom we can walk through life. God didn't design us to live life alone. Scripture is filled with encouragement to grow stronger and be safer through a bond with other believers: "Let us not give up meeting together, as some are in the habit of doing, but let us encourage one another—and all the more as you see the Day approaching" (Heb. 10:25 NIV).

Notes

Chapter 7: Demons Go to Church

1. C. S. Lewis, *The Screwtape Letters* (San Francisco: HarperCollins, 2001), ix.

Chapter 20: I Still Have Questions

1. Barna Group, "Most American Christians Do Not Believe That Satan or the Holy Spirit Exist," April 10, 2009, http://www.barna.org.
2. Gail Goodman, Jianjian Qin, Bette Bottoms, and Phillip Shaver, *Characteristics and Sources of Allegations of Ritualistic Child Abuse* (Washington, DC: National Center on Child Abuse and Neglect, 1995).
3. Maria Puente, "Exorcism Possesses Movie Screens," *USA Today*, April 4, 2011, http://www.usatoday.com.